STOICI

Apply Stoicism to Your Everyday Life

(What Can Stoicism Teach You About the Art of Living)

Nicholas Alvarez

Published by Tomas Edwards

© **Nicholas Alvarez**

All Rights Reserved

ISBN 978-1-989744-77-2

Legal & Disclaimer

The information contained in this book is not designed to replace or take the place of any form of medicine or professional medical advice. The information in this book has been provided for educational and entertainment purposes only.

The information contained in this book has been compiled from sources deemed reliable, and it is accurate to the best of the Author's knowledge; however, the Author cannot guarantee its accuracy and validity and cannot be held liable for any errors or omissions. Changes are periodically made to this book. You must consult your doctor or get professional medical advice before using any of the suggested remedies, techniques, or information in this book.

Upon using the information contained in this book, you agree to hold harmless the Author from and against any damages, costs, and expenses, including any legal fees potentially resulting from the application of any of the information provided by this guide. This disclaimer applies to any damages or injury caused by the use and application, whether directly or indirectly, of any advice or information presented, whether for breach of contract, tort, negligence, personal injury, criminal intent, or under any other cause of action.

You agree to accept all risks of using the information presented inside this book. You need to consult a professional medical practitioner in order to ensure you are both able and healthy enough to participate in this program.

Table of Contents

There are thousands of people trying to find out what Stoicism is. Philosophy is a complex field, and it takes a lot of understanding to grasp it. The philosophies of those that came before us are still influencing the modern day. The Stoic philosophy in particular holds many secrets that can help us tackle the various issues that pop up in our lives.

You probably picked up this book due to its cover, I can't blame you, it does look pretty great. With that being said, you're about to find out it's not just nice looking but this book has everything you were looking for when you thought 'I want to learn about Stoicism.' From its very infancy, who started it and why, to modern thought. What are the criticisms of Stoicism and how have modern-day Stoics fought these back?

Stoicism is a philosophy that has survived since the ancient Greeks for good reason. If you're yearning to learn something new, something that'll let you take control of your life, then let's dive right in.

This book will teach you how to emulate the characteristics of the ancient Stoics. It will imbue you with their wisdom, resilience, self-discipline, confidence, calmness, critical thinking, and decision making. Most importantly, you'll learn how to take full control of your life by using the ancient Stoic's teachings. This journey won't be easy, but I'm confident I can get you through this.

Having spent 10 years studying philosophy, I can safely say that the Stoic philosophy has endured the test of time and is the ideal philosophy to help you take control of your life. It will also ensure that you are the best at dealing with your emotions that you could possibly be.

So, you might be wondering, why should I learn about Stoicism? Well, that's a tough question, mostly because there's just too many reasons to list. But for you, I guess I can try anyways, let me begin with a personal story.

You see, I used to be an extremely shy person. If I could've stayed indoors for the rest of my life, at the time, I would have. I would read books 24/7 or waste my time idly simply waiting for my life to pass. It is a bit of a stretch to even call what I had a life to be honest. Learning Stoicism is actually what introduced a huge twist in my life. Before learning about it, I wasn't up to much, and basically let other people trample over me. After applying Stoic teachings to my life, I became someone. I had a social life, heck, for the first time in my life I had a love life. I opened a side business, and its growth rate shocked me. This gave me time to write, as you can see on the pages of this book. I was able to learn more about various religions and philosophies.

This came as a shock especially to those who knew me well. My family was astounded at the dramatic shift I had introduced in my life. This is what can happen to you too.

I get being skeptical, so let me make you a promise. I promise that this book, by itself, will unlock abilities you didn't even know you had, and not even a week after you've finished it, doors will be opening all around you.

Every second spent in a life of not knowing how to control your mind is another second of your mind being limited and in a jail cell and that is another second of life wasted.

Stop being the person that procrastinates everything, tomorrow is the best liar because today is the real future. Learn to live, be, and thrive in the moment with the teachings of the Stoics. These teachings will help you accomplish any goal on this Earth whether it is getting the dream job or a boost to your career, maybe it's getting the person you fancy or maybe a sporting goal you have in mind, literally anything!

Having a stoic mindset doesn't improve humans, it builds gods.

The stoic teachings that you are about to learn have been used and proven to work for over 2000 years now. In fact, they've only been refined since the days of the ancient Greeks.

Every chapter in this book will provide the reader with either teachings which consist of quotes, strategies or step by step plans to force out old habits and ways of doing things and replace it with valuable key lessons or just general knowledge of stoicism that the reader can gain knowledge from. If you read this book with good attention to detail, then it is likely you will be set for life with a mindset that will enhance your chances of getting what they want out of life and mainly enjoy life in general.

The first step to stop wasting your time, stop procrastinating, and take control of your life is right in front of you, all you need to do, is turn the page.

Stoicism was founded around 2,300 years ago in Ancient Greece, by Zeno of Citium, believed to have been a merchant before studying in Athens. In one sentence, Stoicism is defined as living a life of virtue in accordance with nature. Practicing Stoicism prevents one from experiencing negative emotion as it is a direct result of false reasoning or false values, which are not in accordance with nature and cause suffering and misfortune. This was also held true by the predecessor of Stoicism, which was Cynicism. Zeno was the student of a Cynic and held tightly to the ethical values of this school. Stoic philosophy survived well into the Ancient Roman Culture and had seen several revivals in various forms throughout history. To help you better understand the Stoic school of thought, one must understand the Cynics and the Historical context behind the rise of ascetic lifestyles.

Asceticism broadly encompasses Stoicism, Cynicism and many other modest lifestyles, and is the opposite of Hedonism. Hedonistic behaviors and practices involve overindulgence, drunkenness, frivolity, and greed; in contrast, ascetic practices or lifestyles focus on spiritual growth, which often included abstinence from sexual activity, alcohol, and other secular pleasures. The ascetics of Ancient Greece, including the Cynics and the Stoics, would, to varying extents, live sparse lives with few or no personal possessions. Most refrained from property ownership, and many did not seek social status or political power. Asceticism, in general, has been used in somewhat ambiguous context throughout history, first to describe the sparse means of living practiced by the Cynics, the Stoics, and other like-minded groups. Later on, early incarnations of Christianity, Hinduism, and other religions were considered ascetic due to their practices of sexual abstinence, abstinence from alcohol, fasting, and other strictly disciplined behaviors. In modern times, the Amish lifestyle would be considered ascetic, for they live in society, but keep to themselves, and do not partake in many of the luxuries of the modern world.

Ancient Greek culture was the setting in which schools of thought such as Cynicism and Stoicism were formed, so it is important to understand what it was like to appreciate why the ascetic schools of thought become so popular. Ancient Greece is considered to have been very advanced for its time, in some ways even by modern standards. Many of the ideas that we still use today have roots in Ancient Greece, including Western Philosophy itself, architecture, law, language, theater, and the concept of democracy, to name a few. However, as is the case in any society, the underbelly was not nearly as attractive as the view from the outside. Slavery was a societal norm in Athens for many years, women were not regarded as citizens in the way men were, and Athenians subscribed to a type of Caste system, where members of the lower portion of society were not allowed to vote until later on in the Athenian culture. As time passed and some of these norms changed or were subdued, politics was considered to be the only activity worthy of a citizen, for other, lesser concerns could be delegated to outside parties. The nature of politics being as it is, citizens easily became ensnared in disagreement and corruption and distracted from more important aspects of their lives.

In addition, Athenian culture (and later, Roman Culture), was extremely sexual, in a way that would surely today be considered lewd. In Law, its citizens upheld adultery and philandering as taboo; for example, if a man caught another man in the act of adultery with his wife, it would be within the man's legal rights to kill the other man for his indiscretion. The same standard held for rape. In practice, however, sexual promiscuity was not as taboo as the law made it sound. Prostitution was socially acceptable and constituted a considerable part of the economy. Athenian prostitutes were either young men, or they were women or girls of any age. Both existed primarily for the pleasure of men, for women of status would be looked upon harshly for engaging in what would be considered for them as vulgar acts. While prostitution was commonplace and generally accepted by society, prostitutes and other adulterous women were not allowed to participate in public events or to marry. Phallic statues and the like were featured in prominent places in Athens. This was simply the way things were. However, as is the case with any society, there will always be groups and individuals who do not agree with the customs of the culture, which is how the Cynics and Stoics gained followers simply by not living this way and in the case of the Cynics, actively discouraging the licentiousness which plagued society.

In the context of a society like this: accommodating of sexual promiscuity, politics and all of the deception and disagreement that go along with it, double standards, and hedonistic behavior (cultural aspects that survived well into the later Roman culture), enter the scholar Socrates, known as the father of Western philosophy. Around the fifth century BC, Socrates taught his many students on different subjects, including ethics, logic, theology, and morality. Socrates was and is somewhat of a perplexity of History; despite so many references to him and his work in modern life, there are no written works of Socrates in existence. Everything we know about him today has been gleaned from surviving public records, and from the writings of his followers and students (one of whom, Antisthenes, was the founder of Cynicism.)

Of the many teachings of Socrates, one concept that recurred time and again, no matter the subject, was the concept of virtue. Socrates held many other beliefs that were considered to be radical for his time, for he scoffed at the wealth and political power most citizens aspired to, publicly denounced the democratic political practices of Athens, and rejected pleasures of the flesh as sources of happiness. Instead, Socrates encouraged the pursuit of virtue through community and camaraderie and taught spirituality, morality, logic, and theology. In stark contrast to the society in which they lived, and its permissive, profane norms, Socrates and others like him who condemned this sort of behavior attracted quite a bit of attention, both from disciples and dissenters.

Socrates was one of the first well-known figures in Athenian culture to embrace an ascetic lifestyle, abstaining from decadent behavior and political dealings. He used his logical rhetoric to publicly humiliate prominent men by calling out their morally questionable behaviors. He further stated that logically, a man would not do something which he deemed to be morally wrong. The only two conclusions, then, are that you know that which you do is wrong and continue to do it anyway, or that you engage in these acts without the knowledge that you are doing wrong, in which case you now understand and must not partake in such things any longer. This behavior, in its most extreme form, was the basis of Cynicism. It is also the reason Socrates was tried and publicly executed on charges of corrupting the youth of Athens.

Socrates, Antisthenes and other scholars and philosophers of the time viewed the unhappiness and misfortune which plagued the citizens of Athens as a direct result of their greed, lust and the struggle for power and celebrity. Antisthenes was a scholar of rhetoric before becoming a student of Socrates. He later founded Cynicism as a school of thought by essentially developing Socrates' ideas into an ethical code, and in practice, he lived a similarly minimalist, ascetic life of virtue, and proselytized that others become virtuous by doing the same.

The Cynics held the same beliefs as the later Stoics that a life of virtue in accordance with the will of nature was the path to happiness. However, the Cynics developed radical ideas of what constituted a virtuous life. In accordance with their beliefs, the later Cynics practiced asceticism in a most extreme form, ridding themselves of all but the most basic tools for survival to unburden themselves of the desire for the secular pleasures of society. They rejected their society and cared not for their individual reputations. Instead of removing themselves from society in their rejection of its customs, the Cynics lived in the streets, vehemently evangelizing to the citizens the error of their ways.

The word "Cynic" is rooted in the Ancient Greek word for "dog," as the Cynics were said to live like strays in the streets. The archetypal Cynic you may be familiar with is Diogenes, who often slept in a large ceramic tub in the streets of Athens in a very public attempt to turn poverty into a virtue. Diogenes often drew attention, behaving in ways that were eccentric and controversial. One of these behaviors he is remembered for was carrying a lamp with him in daylight hours, claiming to be in search of an honest man. He was also prone to sleeping and eating anywhere he saw fit, and publicly mocking popular public figures such as Plato and Alexander the Great.

One of Diogenes' followers was Crates of Thebes, who gained notoriety through the act of giving away his fortune to roam the streets as an evangelizing Cynic. Finally, we come to Crates' student, Zeno of Creates, who founded Stoicism based on the ethics of Cynicism. Zeno taught and lived a lifestyle that was in keeping with the Cynical beliefs but behaved in a manner believed by Crates and the other modern Cynics of the time to be far too modest for a Cynic. While Crates instantly recognized Zeno to have an inclination to philosophy, he viewed his student's lack of shamelessness as a flaw. Zeno studied under many other philosophers, and when he began to teach, he kept the ethical code he learned from Crates and the Cynics. However, he did not feel that the ostentatious way the Cynics lived was necessarily the only path to virtue, so he developed a code of ethics for this new, moderate Cynicism and began to teach. Over the years he gained many followers, including the King of Macedonia, who would visit with Zeno whenever he was in the area. Zeno and his followers' interpretations of Cynicism and the code of ethics he developed would later be known as Stoicism.

When discussing Stoicism, we will often talk about the good, the higher good, and what is good for you. Later on, we will also refer to concepts such as goodness and virtue. But then again, isn't passion good for you? Aren't we all told to follow our passion, to pursue it, and to make it our bliss? So, why attempt to be free from it?

This question will be answered here in Chapter 2, as we go into a more in-depth definition of Stoicism. After all, Stoicism is more than a school of thought that tells you to "stoically" endure hardship and bear suffering without complaint. More accurately, its philosophical ideal is to help you achieve "freedom from passion through reason."

To strike while the iron is hot, it's time to discover what passions we refer to and what freedom from passion really means.

What are Whims, Passions and Desires?

The goal of this section is to define what passions are, as well as to differentiate whims, lusts, and desires. Here is our take on all of these terms.

1) **Whims** – A whim is a sudden desire or a fanciful idea. It is a notion which is spontaneous, yet capricious. Thus, you may buy a dress on a whim, or swipe your credit card on the whimsical thought of getting that brand-new gadget.

2) **Lusts** – A lust is a strong desire for something or someone, usually sexual. Aside from lust for sex, there is also lust for riches and lust for power. The wanting is intense and out of control.

3) **Desires** – A desire is a strong feeling of wanting to have something. That something could be a subject (a person), an object, or an outcome. The longing is intense, as is the feeling of excitement at the thought of or in the enjoyment of that something. Remember that an action may or may not be taken on this desire.

4) **Passions** – To a Stoic, passion – or rather passions to be more accurate – are extreme emotions which can become destructive when a person is unable or unwilling to transform them into a higher good.

It doesn't necessarily mean that all passions are bad or that none of them are good. What we should focus on is that passions are unruly emotions which can become self-destructive, especially when they make you lose control. When you let yourself lose control over your thoughts and allow emotions to rule your life, then you will have little to no regard left for the consequences of your actions.

5) **Obsessions** – Still on the extreme, an obsession is an idea (a thought and not a feeling) which continuously preoccupies your mind; it intrudes on your thoughts. Persistent and disturbing, you develop a compulsion towards it, which may be psychologically unhealthy and emotionally harmful or destructive.

As human beings, our passions naturally exist and flow within us. Strong as these desires are, the question is: Shall we entertain them? Will we act on them or not? The answer is up to us, and we hold the key!

As we'll learn in Chapter 4 (Living in Moderation), the key is to moderate our passions and keep them within control. The focus of this control is mostly on those extreme emotions and destructive desires, from which we have to set ourselves free. Stoicism as a way of thinking, therefore, invites you away from the extreme and towards the more moderate way of engaging in positive and productive thoughts.

After having described passions as they are basically understood, the next section is a more in-depth take on what passion is as defined by the Stoics.

How do Stoics Define Passion?

As defined then, during the ancient times, the term **passion** (derived from the Greek word pathos) was used in the sense of pain, anguish, or suffering. To be able to overcome such suffering, one must not only use logic and reason, but also practice apathy.

Apathy (from apatheia) then meant a passive reaction to external events and an indifference to them, on the grounds that no external event is considered good or bad. It is only the inner self (including the inner thought and emotion) which could prove to be either productive or destructive.

These days, however, apathy has lost its real meaning. It now implies a lack of concern and interest or, in general, a lack of emotion. Its indifference also implies a lack of sensitivity to people.

How passions are described

In more recent times, the Stoic viewpoint has become more definitive with how they see passion. Thus, "passion" is more specifically described as:

A fluttering (ptoia) of the soul. Remember, there is tension or disturbance!

An impulse which does not obey the dictates of reason. Thus, it is irrational.

An excessive impulse. It, therefore, goes to the extreme and can be potentially destructive.

A false opinion. A person does not remain passive and indifferent to the stimulus. Assent is given to the impulse to act, and judgment is passed.

From the above viewpoint we've shared, here are some of the impressions we gain:

1) First and foremost, our passions usually have **corporeal** or **bodily** manifestations. For instance, you say that your blood boils when you are angry. Your pulse races and your heart pounds when you are nervous and afraid. In the same way, you say your cup runneth over when you are overflowing with delight. Thus, our passions tend to manifest in the physical sense.

2)	Passions can be **impulsive** and yet **forceful**. Going back to Chrysippus, he clearly illustrated what a runaway passion could equate to. He compared it to a person who is running downhill and is unable to stop himself at will. With the sheer force of the impulse and the strength of it, momentum develops, and it becomes more and more difficult to stop. With a passion of this strength and force, not only is the body driven down, but the soul is also carried away with it.

3)	Since they defy logic and reason, passions can also be **irrational**. Since they are irrational, they can usually be **erroneous**, such as false opinions and hasty judgments. Rein in the irrational passion without letting it prevail, and it will weaken and fade through time.

4)	Likewise, passions can be **extreme**. Since the desire is excessive and extravagant, it defeats the goal of living in moderation. Because the emotions get out of control and become unruly, they cause disquiet within you and ruin your state of inner peace or tranquility.

Why passions need to be controlled

Ideally, your passions are supposed to drive and move you towards the greater good (and that is why we're told to follow our passion), but this isn't always the case. Not everyone has the SELF-CONTROL that's needed to rein-in their passions rationally and reasonably. Young or old, ancient or modern, there are many people who still need to develop self-control first through practice and discipline.

There are a number of passions which drive us to either good or bad, and the four most important passions to control would be distress, fear, lust, and delight.

Below, we've outlined what these four types of passions are and why they need to be controlled:

Distress

DISTRESS is an extreme feeling of anxiety which further causes you sorrow and pain.

Thus, someone who is extremely anxious tends to get easily distressed.

More than a feeling, it is an internal state of stress which keeps compounding, the more you give in to it. Distress can be aggravating, because being in this emotional state can cause physical symptoms and alter your mental and psychological behavior.

Fear

FEAR is an extreme feeling brought on by the belief that something or someone can be dangerous. Fear can be triggered by different factors such as danger, failure, rejection, change, and even the unknown.

The less fearful you grow in life, the more you discover that most of your fears are false and unfounded. Much of them are based on false beliefs which we've mistakenly come to accept. Thus, it helps to understand, face, and control these fears.

Lust

LUST is something which we've already discussed. Again, it's an extreme feeling of urgent wanting, usually power-related or sexual in nature. It is possible, however, to replace lustful feelings with productive thoughts and to distract your attention away from the source.

Delight

DELIGHT is an extreme feeling of pleasure over something which you crave and long for. As a source of pleasure, it does absorb a lot of your attention, thus, causing you to feel giddy and distracted. The happiness, though, doesn't last and you begin to seek more.

Therefore, delight also comes in the form of thrill seeking. There is an intense desire to be out there and seek new abilities and more experiences. Regardless of expense or danger, the longing never stop. You will always be after the next best experience, with the current one no longer being enough.

What these passions lead to

Distress, Fear, Pleasure, and Appetite or Lust are all overwhelming passions which lead to reckless, irrational responses. Pleasure and distress are usually experienced in the present, while fear and lust are projected into the future.

As a vexation, Distress disturbs you in different forms. It can lead to you develop negative feelings which come in the guise of jealousy, envy, malice. It also manifests in the form of worry, anxiety, annoyance, pity, anguish, sorrow, and grief.

With the unreasonable expectation of something bad about to happen, fear grows and feeds upon itself. The perceived threat can cause feelings of panic, fright, dread, and terror. Along with fear comes the experience of shame, agony, superstition, and paranoia.

As an unreasonable reaching out or scrambling for something good, a lusty appetite is associated with wanting, yearning, and longing. Off the charts in your sexual and non-sexual craving, you will experience anger, wrath, selfishness, and greed, like a hunger which cannot be satisfied.

Out of over-elation or extreme pleasure, it could lead you to personal strife. Always, there will be a endless struggle for more self-gratification, and this becomes habitual. You are enchanted by what you see as sources of happiness (or so they seem) and disenchanted with life when you are without them. You learn to be happy at the expense of other people and to rejoice at the misfortune of others, because, by then, your passions will have been all mixed up.

When you are controlled by your passions, you can get trapped in this whirlwind of emotions. At times, they can cause you such agony and pain, that the suffering becomes self-inflicted. Thus, to spare you from the destructive effect of extreme emotions, you have to establish SELF-CONTROL.

Of these [three areas of study], the principle, and most urgent, is that which has to do with the passions; for these are produced in no other way than by the disappointment of our desires, and the incurring of our aversions. It is this that introduces disturbances, tumults, misfortunes, and calamities; and causes sorrow, lamentation and envy; and renders us envious and jealous, and thus incapable of listening to reason.

- Epictetus (Discourses 3.2.3, trans. Hard)

What does Freedom from Passion Mean?

Because Stoicism is often defined as a philosophy and a way of life, many people overlook the fact that it is also an ethical doctrine. Thus, there is such a thing as STOIC DOCTRINE. This ethical doctrine promotes the ultimate goal (as we've mentioned) of attaining "freedom from passion through reason."

What it means to be passion-free

"Freedom from passion" does not necessarily mean the absence of emotion, or a lack of it. It does not mean being void of emotion or, in other words being "emotionless" or "emotionally flat".

It is not a lack of care or concern, either. Thus, a true Stoic cannot be faulted as being uncaring or unconcerned, quiet though they may be. Although it is termed as an indifference (and most people are shocked by the use of this term), do not be taken aback, because it is more about being indifferent to the four types of passions, especially when they lead you to the bad.

Being indifferent to these passions means not judging them to be either good or bad. This is irrelevant to a Stoic, because what matters is that these passions are neither extreme nor destructive. If it helps, come to understand your emotions like changes in the weather. With its highs and lows, there are days when the weather can be good or bad. There are times when the skies are downcast and it's stormy outside, but this shouldn't stop you from being free to do what you have to and going on with your life.

What freedom from passion is

When you are able to weather all kinds of emotions, this in itself is freedom from passion. You experience and enjoy a more stable emotional life. You are able to form an appropriate emotional response to a person or situation.

Whether the impulses are desirable or undesirable as they come, the emotions are moderated, and the responses are held in check. As a Stoic, your emotional responses are not regretful and melodramatic. Thus, you avoid sorrows and troubles which, as we've said, earlier, are often self-inflicted. We bring these negative emotions upon ourselves, simply because we allow them to affect us and then those around us.

Aside from WEATHERING a variety of emotions, this freedom also means ENDURING the experience of hardship in the face of passion (or suffering). There is equanimity or evenness of temperament during the highs and lows, the ups and downs of life, such that balance is always restored from within.

In line with balance, freedom from passion also requires MODERATING one's passions. One should not yield to their passions or allow their desires to fuel obsessions.

How freedom is achieved individually

The ultimate goal of STOIC FREEDOM is "freedom from suffering." Initially, such freedom can be achieved by first establishing self-control or, in or other words, control over one's passions in order to attain inner calm and clear judgment. Eventually, this self-control can be improved by learning to be attentive to the present moment and using your logic in dealing with the current circumstances.

In the long run, it is this inner self-control which would help you overcome extreme desires and destructive emotions. Thus, it is not all emotions which Stoicism aspires to extinguish, but rather those destructive ones which make life more complicated and difficult.

As to the importance of being calm and rational, it is only through logic (or logos) that one can clearly understand the true nature of the universe and the natural, universal reason behind all things. Thus, Stoics are encouraged to "live according to nature", meaning according to the natural laws of the universe, as well as our own human nature which is governed by LOGIC and REASON.

So, instead of complaining and frustrating over the external circumstances which are beyond your control, a Stoic philosophy prompts you to examine your own judgment and behavior. Assess yourself, in order to determine where you could have possibly diverged (or been distracted from) the universal reason of things, or of nature in general.

What this freedom means universally

Freedom from passion works, not only on a personal level but also on a universal one. As a way of life, Stoicism challenges all of us to "live according to nature." Existentially, this means discovering how we each fit into the universe and learning how we all can coexist in oneness and harmony with each other. The STOIC PATH may not be easy (and that is why you are prepared for hardship), but it ultimately leads to a life full of joy and tranquility.

At this point, it helps to be reminded that the philosophy of Stoicism was born, not at the best and most prosperous of times. Quite the opposite, it came at the most challenging of times in ancient Greco-Roman history.

Be reminded that it was then a time of war and crisis. A few decades earlier, the famous Alexander the Great had prematurely died and his conquests had ended. The times were uncertain, and good leadership was badly needed.

The Stoic way of thinking was an answer to the times. It was not an escapist theory. It did not promise that there would be no more hardship and suffering for people, or that there would be more abundance and wealth for everyone. Again, there was no reassurance either that progress would be quick to achieve.

In fact, by now, most of us clearly understand that the Stoic path is the more difficult choice to make, the more challenging life to take! But, if it intends to liberate people from suffering from outward things they can't control and inspires people to focus inward on what they can control, then wouldn't this freedom from unruly, pent-up passions benefit the universe in some significant way?

Thus, in a world whose morals are gradually deteriorating and falling apart, there is a way to possibly rebuild what remains of our strength and virtue. In typical Stoic fashion of thinking that bad can be transformed into good and that good always prevails over evil, then a revival of Stoicism in the modern world could, once again, provide an answer.

Although the way of thinking of Stoicism has won admirers from Renaissance through to now, a ton has been said about the fact that it is so imperative to have the option to encounter discretion and to be reliable. Usually, these are two amazingly significant capacities to have in life.

If one can't control themselves, it will be a test for them to accomplish anything beneficial. Instead, they will, in all likelihood, become involved with endless diversions and technicalities.

An Analogy

One way to comprehend what can occur, if someone has no control, can be to envision a child in a toy shop. In one minute they will be attracted to one area and, in a matter of seconds, they will be drawn to another area.

This child won't most likely adhere to any one area, which will prevent them from getting a comprehension of anything. The reason being is that when they start to focus on one toy, they will end up observing another toy and before long end up leaving.

A Wasted life

To carry on along these lines as a grown-up is going to prevent one from having the option to adhere to anything. Much the same as a child in a toy shop; they can start something and afterward cast it aside not long after.

This can affect their profession, alongside different areas of their life. For instance, if one can control themselves, it is in all probability going to be a test for them to act reasonably and to practice all the time.

Where has everything gone?

One could then think back on their life and wonder what they have been doing; it might appear as if life has quite recently cruised by. Their emotions and their contemplations will at that point have controlled them, instead of one having the option to deal with these pieces of their being.

Without the ability to hold their considerations and feelings within proper limits, it will have negatively affected their life. One will resemble a little vessel that is hurled around the sea, not a significant ship that can handle pretty much anything.

The Other Part

What's more, if one can't prop up during the setbacks that emerge, it is likewise impossible that they will accomplish anything significant. When things warm up, as it were, they will drop out.

They may be genuinely enormous assembled or they may not, however, what they won't have is the internal muscle that will empower them to continue onward. Someone like this will need a simple life, not the solidarity to handle the difficulties that life brings.

Another Analogy

This will resemble setting off to a rec center and not having any desire to lift anything that is excessively overwhelming. This will make it simpler for them to lift things, yet what it won't do is enable someone to end up more grounded.

It could then be said that they will squander their time and that it may have been exceptional if they had remained at home. Considering, the being able to endure pain is crucial.

The Dark Side

In any case, while being aloof will enable one to handle life, it can have a negative effect if it is taken to the extreme. Or, then again, to be increasingly exact; this can be something that happens because of someone's understanding of being unemotional.

Through reading up omit, someone can accept that they have to deny how they feel to command their emotions fundamentally. Their psyche is then going to be in a consistent fight with their body.

One Dimensional

Being like this may enable them to push ahead and to accomplish their objectives, yet it can likewise set them up to have issues when it comes to connecting with others. Their emotions, the things that will enable them to connect to other people and for others to connect to them, will be pushed down.

They are then going to be human, yet they may seem to be however they don't generally feel anything. This would then be able to set them up to have an in all respects desolate presence, and what they accomplish likely won't fill this hole.

A Deeper Look

What someone like this may discover is that they didn't have a decent association with their emotions in the first place, with this being the motivation behind why they were attracted to stoicism. Or then again why they came to accept that carrying on thusly was what it intended to be, unemotional.

One could then keep on denying how they feel and accept that they were making the best choice. This would have provided them with approval that they expected to keep reality under control: that they are maintaining a strategic distance from how they feel.

Way Back

This can demonstrate that they are conveying a great deal of pain because of what occurred during their initial years. Maybe this was when they didn't get the consideration that they required to build up a sound association with their emotions.

As of now, in their life, pushing their emotions down would have been a way for them to handle the pain they were in. Because of what they encountered; it would have added in all probability enabled them to have the option to manage a considerable measure of pain.

Mindfulness

If one had an early childhood where they needed to disconnect from their emotions and had no other decision than to endure intolerable pain, it won't be a shock if they are attracted to 'stoicism.' This type of stoicism is then necessarily going to be another protection that one will use to keep away from their inward injuries.

If one can identify with this, and they need to turn into an incorporated individual, they may need to connect for outside help. This is something that can be provided with the help of an advisor or a healer, for example.

Cognitive Behavioral Therapy - Stoicism and Medication

As a matter of first importance, Social Anxiety Disorder/Social Phobia is the dread, or if nothing else the sentiment of inconvenience, of being around other people. That is the clarification of the disease in its broadest sense. There are numerous other specific fears identified with Social Anxiety Disorder (S.A.D.). Yet, our concerning this segment is to take a gander at the different, adequate treatments accessible.

The main answer is psychotherapy, and the primary strategy in this regard is Cognitive Behavioral Therapy. I realize we've talked about this previously. However, I need to come at it from a somewhat different edge and clarify why it's so reliable and far speedier in demonstrating results than various forms of therapy. There are two fundamental reasons.

Right off the bat, when the specialist and the patient meet just because they go to a collective choice concerning what extent the treatment will last. So straight away, they set an objective. It's been discovered that the usual number of sessions a patient has with C.B.T. is sixteen.

Besides, contrast this with analysis, which may take years.

C.B.T. is a genuinely extreme, informative program and depends in no little part on homework. The patient must do his or her part for the therapy to demonstrate appropriately effective. Accepting that the sessions are week after week, at that point toward the finish of every session, the patient has certain activities to do to set herself up for her next session. Important number of different forms of therapy, subsequently, the course of treatment isn't open-finished.

Thirdly, a few specialists pursue the old apathetic line of treatment. Fundamentally, this expresses if you have a problem, you have one problem. At that point, you begin stressing and worrying;

46

this is another problem. Presently, you have two issues. Try to acknowledge this problem serenely and work it out. Try not to lounge around stressing over it. Accomplish something. Worrying isn't doing anything, except diving you deeper and deeper into a dump from which in the long run there could be no way out.

The principal thing a psychotherapist ought to do is to guarantee the patient that she gets no opportunity of recuperating from S.A.D. or then again, any tension-based condition by her resolve. How frequently have we heard; "Goodness, please, wake up." Or; "Suck it up. We, as a whole, have problems." Patients ought to be clarified of this speculation directly from the word 'go.'

I realize that previously, I've said that I'm no admirer of meds. What these medications will do to you in the long haul is still, to a great extent, obscure. This is especially legitimate when you think about that different medications suit different people. Is anything but an instance of 'one size fits all.' That being stated, notwithstanding, if an individual is enduring intensely, maybe near suicide, such is their perspective, at that point, some medication must be regulated to quiet them down.

The three fundamental sorts are Anxiolytics, Beta-blockers, and Antidepressants. Anxiolytics come in the forms of Xanax, Klonopin or Clonazepam, and Diazepam or Valium. Antidepressants we can name straightaway. These come in the forms of Sertraline, which is Zoloft, Bupropion, which is Wellbutrin and Duloxetine, the name for Cymbalta.

Stoicism for Trauma, Chronic Conditions and General Health and Wellness

Stoicism is an old way of thinking that was built up in ancient Greece by Zeno of Cilium which prospered all through Greece and later that of the Roman Empire. Those managing injury frequently experience serious difficulties managing everyday life and particularly recuperating profoundly, sincerely and rationally, from horrible accidents.

The equivalent applies to those living with constant health conditions. Those with endless health conditions frequently manage a great deal, going from dismissal, insulting, analysis, and notwithstanding tormenting from others just as maintaining the health problems themselves.

Rationally, profoundly and genuinely, it is challenging to manage constant health conditions. There is regularly plenty of misfortunes as it requires some investment to discover the root causes and treat them. Likewise, it requires some investment for individuals to honestly acknowledge it also, either on an individual level or for those around you. Stoicism is a reasonable way of thinking for those managing emotional issues, for example, continual health conditions.

By utilizing stoicism and tolerating your conditions when managing perpetual health conditions, it enables oneself to turn out to progressively target and search for more approaches to improve their health yet, besides, their life.

Now and again, of which I have managed by and by it tends to be simple for one to turn out to be unpleasant, angry and skeptical because of the abuse of those with eternal health conditions.

Stoic meditations, reflections, and philosophical thoughts can frequently be combined with other profound or physical activities to help mend sincerely just as rationally and profoundly from awful encounters when managing constant health conditions.

Regardless of the sad conditions of endless health conditions, it doesn't need to ruin someone's life and their viewpoint of life. Truth be told, through managing hardships we frequently find (or rediscover) the best in ourselves and become an all the more well-rounded and better individual as a result of it.

Stoic week is an incredible point to begin to learn and apply the establishments of stoicism to your life. From that point, you can start to discover more books and online assets to support you. I locate the day by day morning and evening meditation to be useful.

Learn the Power of Becoming a True Stoic Male

A few things are in our control and others not. Thoughts as we would like to think, interest, want, abhorrence, and, in a word, whatever are our actions. Things not in our control are body, property, notoriety, direction, and, in a single word, whatever are not our actions.

You are born in this beautiful, strange planet which is as it should be. Your family, relatives, mother, and father celebrated the introduction of a male in this world. A youngster is developed by sustenance, support from his folks - mother, adores him gives her life for him, father employments, in any case, is a remarkable one, where we have to turn into. Dauntless, the gallant, discipline his child, so that, he can figure out how to master the genuine manly power. There are situations, where the tyke loses his father, because of unexpected yet avoidable/unavoidable condition, which transforms the youthful tyke into a defiant, presumptuous grown-up! This section is for that blackguard who lost his father or for the person who anticipates that his father should comprehend the complexities of human connections and live for once a solid male!

Who is a Stoic? Also, how to turn into the True Male.

"Stoic" is a word to portray a person, who shows fewer feelings, or who talks less. Stoicism was polished, as a way of life by Epictetus - who was born as a slave in Hierapolis, Phrygia, present-day Turkey. Epictetus figured out how to apply the Stoic standards, and never regretted on the difficulties tossed at him. His master, at one case, wound his leg, but then, he grinned and told his master in a calm tone; "See, I disclosed to you my leg would break." Through Epictetus, we can create and develop the propensity for turning into a True Stoic Male.

Presently, as we start examining, and slashing the practices on turning into a Stoic male, we should inspect now somewhat profound on who this person is. Regardless of whether you'd like this new change in your character, personality, your folks, companions, relatives, may see you as egotistical, However, you will be loaded up with calmness, tranquility calling every one of the Gods, gathering you the power to master any situations, condition, and just controlling your thoughts and actions. That is a power you should learn and follow. The following are a couple of pills taken from Epictetus' lessons. You should bite and swallow regular! These pills are not delectable, yet they are here to give you the total power inside yourself, and not depending on others for your weakness, situations which your see are crazy.

Let Death and outcast, and every single other thing which seems horrendous be day by day before your eyes, yet necessarily Death, and you will never engage any miserable idea, nor too anxiously want anything

Life is a battle. You can't escape now, and just Death is the way. Terrifying yet, this is the last answer before leaving Earth. We are in pursuit of our wants - money, vocation, ladies, desire, power, extraordinary house, connections. All these outer things are neither terrible nor useful for a Stoic. All these appear to be indifferent to a Stoic. If somebody discovers this person who lost his money, dismissed by a lady, and is so calm as water, he will begin asking - why is this person is so cold, or refreshing, untethered from this reality. If ever a situation appears to be crazy, envision how God Zeus might take control of the situation. That is the thing that Epictetus said to his understudies while he was encouraging Stoicism back in Rome.

Token Mori (recall, one day you also beyond words)

There is no real way to put this yet recollect; your time is running out! In this way, what should a Stoic Male accomplish that guarantees him not to append anything outside and have full oversight over himself? Get yourself a Goal! You need a mission right presently to challenge yourself. Hit the Gym today, and fabricate your build, lift the weight, and eat that torment, since Stoic is indifferent to agony and joy. Need to construct another skill, practice every day like you loathe doing, meet individuals, get familiar with their shrouded expectations, read their small-scale inconspicuous feelings, figure out how to be calm like a stone, talk less, let your actions do the talking. Your time is constrained, so realize where to invest your energy - Decoding individuals, mastering a new skill, or attempting to assemble your definitive structure.

Be generally quiet, or say only what is essential, and in few words.

Guarantee not to permit your giggling to be excessive; on numerous events, nor bountiful like a lunatic. Indeed, this is extremely difficult. We, as a whole, prefer to split on - cruel jokes, and this can help the state of mind. What's more, this is one power you can use in your life. State if your manager put-down or your dear companion sold out despite your good faith or your cherished one spits at you. You can back with your Amused Mastery, and as though, you discovered what sort of person he/she was. Concur and Amplifying to situations, for example, considering you a Bastard, pointless, and reframing to your world gives you another power wherein you can rehearse.

If a person gave your body to any more peculiar, he met on his way, and you would unquestionably be irate. Also, do you feel no disgrace in giving over your very own brain to be confounded and mystified by any individual who happens to ambush you verbally?

At long last your quietness, your words amount to nothing if you couldn't close a bonehead with your word. A genuine Stoic like Cato, utilizes his words sparingly. Why, since you lose any fight if you have to demonstrate your value. Cato's Action did the talking. He was prepared to execute himself to oust Julius Caesar from the position of authority (which he in the long run achieved)

We are working up a resilient person who lost his expectations, dreams from the truth, learning while at the same time teaching ourselves to grasp the power of manliness swimming through your veins and feel an absolute control living inside you. Keep in mind this: What stays in this world is your inheritance. The amount of value you are as a person. If you need to test an absolute power between human interactions, begin perusing the 48 laws of power. Those are a portion of the genuine thick pills to swallow!

If you are new to Stoicism, knowing the key players is very important because their influence and teachings are equally important to your ability to use the Stoic philosophy to improve every aspect of your life.

Before we start doing that, it is worth noting that stoicism does not discriminate, which is why popular ancient Stoics were from diverse cultural backgrounds. Of the famous ancient stoics we know and will discuss, one was an emperor, another a water carrier, another a slave, and yet another a playwright. Others were soldiers, senators, and other independently wealthy. Stoicism, a focus on the internal state: thoughts, beliefs, and actions, is what connects all stoics.

This chapter is a short biographical account of the most important ancient stoics. By understanding these key figures, you will avoid feeling too lost as we discuss the history of stoicism in the next chapter.

1: Zeno of Citium

Bust of Zeno of Citium

Zeno of Citium appears first on our list not because he is the most notable of all the stoics, but because he takes the credit for being the originator of modern day stoicism. His story is also one of the most interesting ones.

He was a merchant who, once as he was travelling between Phoenicia and Peiraeus, a turbulent sea shipwrecked him. He lost his consignment and ended up stranded in Athens where upon wandering into a bookstore, he met Socrates who introduced him to the stoic philosophy and much later, Crates, the Athenian philosopher. Out of the influences of Socrates and Crates, Zeno developed the principles and values that we now call stoicism.

Zeno did not see his shipwrecking as a bad omen. On the contrary, according to Diogenes, he considered the shipwreck the wakeup call he needed to start living a good life. As Diogenes once, Zeno was fond of jokingly saying:

"Now that I've suffered shipwreck, I'm on a good journey…" "…You've done well, fortune, driving me thus to philosophy."

Zeno of Citium

As he learned more about philosophy and started implementing it in his life, he started teaching it at the Stoa Poilike, with the philosophy at first called Zenoism, which his followers later changed to Stoicism.

The restored Stoa of Attalos in Athens

Although the stoicism Zeno taught at the Stoa Poilike and the one we practice today are different, the underlying principles and teachings remain largely unchanged, only better explained for practical implementation in one's life. Zeno taught the most important stoic philosophy: that happiness or human wellness comes from living in accordance with nature and reason.

Like other philosophers of his time, none of the writings of Zeno of Citium survived. Most of what we know about him and the early stoics that contributed greatly to the development of modern day stoicism—Cleanthes and Chrysippus—is from Diogenes's work, Lives and Opinions of Eminent Philosophers.

2: Cleanthes of Assos

Bust of Cleanthes

Cleanthes succeeded Zeno to become the second leader of the stoic philosophy/movement.

Birthed at Assos, Diogenes notes that Cleanthes arrived in Athens with four Drachma (early coins), and before attending lecturers offered by Zeno, was a boxer known to attend the lectures of Crates the Cynic.

In a new city with no means of income other than boxing, which was seasonal, devoted to the pursuit of wisdom, and the study of philosophy, he became a "professional" water-carrier, which is how he got his nickname, the "Well-Water-Collector", and the income he needed to fuel his pursuit of knowledge and wisdom. The Roman court did not like this. Through summons, the court asked him to explain why he did not work and instead spent his day studying philosophy. He explained himself by working hard during the night. The court, now amazed by his industriousness, offered him money, but at the advice of Zeno, Cleanthes refused the offer.

After Zeno passed on, Cleanthes became the leader of the stoic school, a post he held for 32 years and used to pass on his knowledge. Chrysippus is his most notable student.

"When someone inquired of him what lesson he ought to give his son, Cleanthes in reply quoted words from the Electra: Silence, silence, light be thy step."

Diogenes, The Lives and Opinions of Eminent Philosophers

3: Marcus Aurelius

Bust of Marcus Aurelius

Marcus Aurelius is an influential ancient stoic. Born to a prominent family, he grew upon to become a Roman Emperor. Although little information exists about his childhood life, the existing texts paint a picture of a serious young man who enjoyed hunting, wrestling, and boxing.

How Marcus Aurelius ascended into emperorship is somewhat by chance. Text shows that nearing his death, Hadrian,

Emperor of Rome from 117 to 138 CE, named senator Antoninus Pius as his successor with the condition being that to ascend to the throne, Antoninus, then childless, had to adopt Marcus Aurelius. Antoninus Pius was emperor from 138 to 161 CE; upon his death, Marcus ascended to the throne.

Marcus ruled Rome from 161-180 CE. Although many historians and philosophers consider him one of the five good Roman emperors, his reign was far from smooth. During his reign, the Roman Empire fought against the Parthian Empire, barbarians attacking its northern border, and had to deal with a devastating plague and the growing popularity of Christianity.

During his reign, being Emperor of Rome was the most powerful post in the world— much like POTUS—and as such, Marcus wielded immense power. That despite the power he wielded, power that could allow him to fulfil any of his desires and inclinations, Marcus is one of the most impactful of all Roman emperors is proof that when applied well, stoicism can be life changing.

As illustrated in his Daily Meditations, the diary he kept, we see a man clearly guided by wisdom and virtue as he went about fulfilling his empiric duties. Though his private Journal—the Meditations—we see a man who concentrated his life on being more virtuous, honest, humble, wise, self-disciplined, and sage-like and therefore impervious to external elements and temptations.

Most stoic teachings on inner strength, personal ethics, self-actualization, and self-discipline are from Marcus Aurelius teachings as illustrated in his Meditations, a must read book for all Stoic.

4: Lucius Annaeus Seneca

Bust of Seneca

Seneca the Younger, commonly called Seneca, ranks second on the list of prominent and influential of the ancient stoics. Born in the Southern of Spain to Seneca the Elder, a revered Roman writer, Seneca the Younger schooled in Rome and later pursued a career in politics where he managed to rise to the rank of a financial clerk, a regarded position. Coming from a wealthy family, he was independently wealthy—one of the richest in ancient Rome—and a prominent playwright.

Accused of sleeping with the emperor's niece, Claudius, the Roman Emperor from AD 41 to 54, exiled Seneca the Younger— in 41 A.D—to the island of Corsica. From exile, Seneca the Younger penned a letter addressed to his mother in which he tried to console her during his exile. Eight years after Claudius exiled him, his wife, Agrippina, sought permission to have Seneca freed from exile and allowed to become an adviser and tutor of Nero, a future emperor known for his tyranny and notoriety. Coincidentally, in 65 A.D., Nero accused Seneca of plotting against him and ordered his execution.

There is no doubt that the life of Seneca the Younger was turbulent—much like our modern lives. Throughout his many troubles in life, Stoic teachings and principles taught to him by Attalus, one of his earliest teachers, gave him the constant strength he needed to persevere.

From his writing, we also know that Seneca the Younger also drew inspiration from Marcus Porcius Cato Uticensis commonly referred to as Cato the Younger.

The most notable of his writing is Letters from a Stoic. The text offers highly actionable philosophical nuggets of wisdom on religion, wealth, handling grief, as well as how to become a man/woman of action.

5: Hecato of Rhodes

"Believe me it is better to understand the balance-sheet of one's own life than of the corn trade." "We are not given a short life but we make it short, and we are not ill-supplied but wasteful of it." "Think your way through difficulties: harsh conditions can be softened, restricted ones can be widened, and heavy ones can weigh less on those who know how to bear them."

Seneca the Younger

Although Seneca drew influence from many other stoic philosophers such as Epicurus and Cato the Younger, his writings quote Hecato (or Hecaton) of Rhodes the most.

Hecato was a respected writer who wrote treaties but despite having many treaties to his name, none of his written work survived.

6: Epictetus

Bust of Epictetus

Epictetus is a highly influential ancient stoic. Compared to Marcus Aurelius and Seneca, both of whom were very close to the Roman throne, one as an emperor and the other as an advisor to a future emperor, Epictetus's societal standing is very different.

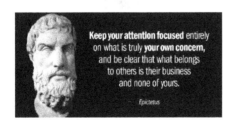

Keep your attention focused entirely on what is truly your own concern, and be clear that what belongs to others is their business and none of yours.

Epictetus

"Let death and exile, and all other things which appear terrible, be daily before your eyes, but death chiefly; and you will never entertain any abject thought, nor too eagerly covet anything."

Epictetus

Born as a slave into the opulent household of Epaphroditus of Hierapolis, Epictetus discovered philosophy when his master gave him permission to study liberal arts; he learned under the tutelage of Musonius Rufus, a revered Stoic of the time.

Shortly after the death of Nero the tyrannical emperor, Epictetus sought his freedom from slavery and after getting it, became a philosophy teacher in Rome where he taught for 20+ years until the

Domitian, the Roman Emperor from 81 to 96 A.D. banished all philosophers. He sought refuge in Nicopolis Greece, which is where, after establishing a school, he taught Stoic philosophy until his demise.

Most notable stoic quotes are from Epictetus. Moreover, his influence permeates the teachings of other equally influential stoic philosophers such as Marcus Aurelius. Unlike other stoics, Epictetus did not write things down. Most of what we know about him and his core teaching come from the notes of Arrian, one of his students. Despite never having written anything himself, his teachings have been influential in the lives of many a great men. Reading his quotes is likely to offer you guidance and be fodder for the self-growth and development you need in your life at any given moment.

7: Gaius Musonius Rufus

Bust of Gaius Musonius

Remembered as a teacher to Epictetus, Gaius Musonius Rufus, the son of Capito, a Roman eques—a knight—, was born in Volsinii, Etruria around 20-30 AD.

Before Nero the tyrannical Roman emperor ascended to the throne, Gaius Rufus was a prominent philosopher and stoic teacher. After ascending to the throne, Nero became obsessed with conspiracy theories and fearing for his life and dethroning him, he accused Musonius of participating in the Pisonian conspiracy and banished him to Gyaruss, a desolate island on the Aegean Sea.

After the death of Nero when Rome was under the leadership of Gaba, Musonius returned to Rome only for Titus Flavius Vespasianus, the Roman Empire from 69–79 AD to banish all philosophers in 71 AD but Musonius in 75 AD. He returned to Rome after the death of Vespasianus and died there around 101 AD.

Musonius taught practical philosophy: how to use philosophical teachings to live a great life. He taught the principles of living a virtuous and good life as the ultimate path to human happiness and wellbeing.

Centuries after his demise, Origen, a Greek scholar, noted that Musonius and Socrates were the best examples of how to live the best life.

All of us are so fashioned by nature that we can live our lives free from error and nobly.

-Musonius Rufus

8: Cato the Younger

Bust of Cato the Younger

Many historians and philosophers consider Cato the Younger someone who lived a stoic life governed by stoic principles and values. Like Epictetus, Cato the Younger did not write any substantive stoic texts. How he chose to live his life and undertake his daily actions, however, was highly influential in the philosophical sense in existence back then.

Born into a well to do family of notable political leaders, Cato the Younger spent most of his life in servitude of the masses;

in addition to being a stoic philosopher, he was also a soldier, an aristocrat and a Roman Senator.

As one of the most notable Optimate, a group of traditionalists who sought to preserve the old Roman constitution and system of Governorship, Cato the Younger was a vehement critic of Julius Caesar and his leadership to a point where he would at times act as the leader of the opposition.

Out of his opposition of Julius Caesar and his devotion to his incorruptible morals and support of the Optimates, when Cato the Younger learned that Caesar would triumph at the Battle at Thapsus in 46 B.C. and become Emperor of Rome, he chose to commit suicide.

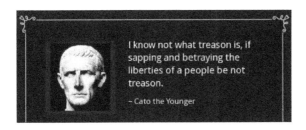

I know not what treason is, if sapping and betraying the liberties of a people be not treason.

– Cato the Younger

The story of Cato the Younger as told in Cato: A Tragedy in Five Acts, a popular play in Ancient Rome—especially how, out of principle, he took his life to avoid living under the rule of Julius Caesar—inspired many a great men of the day who quoted Cato the Younger in their public and private speeches. It also inspired great men of later generations.

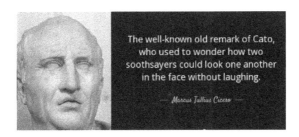

The well-known old remark of Cato, who used to wonder how two soothsayers could look one another in the face without laughing.

— Marcus Tullius Cicero —

It inspired George Washington and the revolutionary war, Benjamin Franklin who used lines from the play as his motto and the opening lines in his diary, and John and Abigail Adams whose love letters to each other had quotes from Cato the Younger.

Although he was quiet and reserved, Cato the Younger is one of the most stoic of all stoic philosophers of his time, thereafter, and even to date. He was very fond of saying:

"I begin to speak only when I'm certain what I'll say isn't better left unsaid."

Cato the Younger

The life of Cato the Younger is full of lessons that every stoic should adopt, internalize, and practice daily. The Quote above is a great example. We should all aim to speak only when what we have to say is important enough to say. If something is not true, helpful, inspiring, necessary, or kind, we should not say it.

Since its initial establishment, stoicism has developed greatly. The next chapter looks at the rich history of stoicism.

'We are more often frightened than hurt, and we suffer more in imagination than in reality.'- Seneca

Ponder on the aforementioned quote for a while and then analyze your life and that of others in reference to it. You will be amazed at how true it is for it is indeed living in our imagination and disregarding the present that brings pain and suffering. If only we start living in the present and in harmony with will we live a happier, more meaningful life. Let's see how you can actualize that.

Why Live in Harmony with Nature

All branches of philosophy believe that our goal in life is to achieve 'Eudaimonia', which is translated as 'a good, meaningful life.' According to Stoicism, Eudaimonia can be attained by living in complete agreement and accordance with nature.

This was the main slogan of all Stoic leaders.

Human beings, as Stoics believe are rational animals and this ability to think rationality is what distinguishes us from beasts and all the other living beings. We are indeed different and superior to other living species on Earth for this very reason, the ability to think logically. This is how nature designed us and if we wish to live a good life, a life that helps us attain Eudaimonia, we need to learn to unlock and understand our ability to think rationally so we can actually behave as rational beings and live in complete harmony with nature.

Often, we come across incidents wherein we see people behaving cruelly, irrationally and barbarically with others. We see people betraying, fighting, cursing, hating and nurturing ill sentiments for one another. Sadly, often we accept it as natural human behavior and let go of it while condemn some acts. What we fail to understand is that such behaviors are not natural and acceptable because they do not conform to the laws of nature. We are designed to behave in agreement with nature and not go against it. All the inhuman acts we engage in make us live in disagreement with nature.

Instead of quarrelling with one another and disregarding rationality, we need to understand that we are born to live as rational beings and it is only by doing this that we can abide by nature and live a truly meaningful life. We are meant to live like humans, not animals and that is how we can live in acceptance with nature.

To live like rational humans, it is important to follow another important stoic principle that focuses on living by virtue.

What Does it Mean to Live by Virtue

According to Stoics, attaining virtue is achieving the highest good by excelling in terms of living like a rational human being so you can then achieve Eudaimonia. As there are different types of virtue as classified by Stoics, we can excel in different ways. According to Stoicism, there are four cardinal virtues:

Prudence or Wisdom: This comprises of good judgment, good sense, being able to see things from different perspectives and excellent deliberation.

Fortitude or Courage: This includes perseverance, bravery, confidence, honesty and authenticity.

Fairness or Justice: This comprises of public service, benevolence, fair dealing and good heartedness.

Temperance or Self-Discipline: This includes self-control, humility, forgiveness and orderliness.

By acting according to these 4 virtues, you start to shape yourself as a rational, intellectual being who knows how to distinguish between right and wrong, and can practice that to achieve a good life. Hence, the key to attain Eudaimonia is to work on building these four virtues as these are the tools to become a rational being.

In the truest Stoic sense, you have to work on practicing all the virtues listed above to become completely virtuous. Working on one or two will not turn you into a rational being that lives in agreement with nature. If you have good sense and judgment, but are not just and benevolent then you cannot always practice good judgment because there will come a time when your biasness will cloud your ability to think rationally and make you make an unbiased decision. So what is it that you need to do to practice all the virtues and live in agreement with nature? Let's find that out.

How to Become Virtuous and Live in Harmony with Nature

While there are several things you need to do to become virtuous, here a few good places to start:

When having a discussion with someone, try to keep as many angles into perspectives as possible. When you feel like becoming fixated on one viewpoint, think of how many other angles are associated with it. One good way of doing that is by talking to people with diverse opinions and jotting down different ideas as you move along.

Accept different ideas with respect and warmth and always remember how it is our right to think freely and hold different opinions. You can obviously disagree with others but when you have to, do so with respect. Keep your opinions to yourself and try not to shove them on to others.

When dealing with people, in a business or where money matters are involved, do so with fairness. Remember 'as you sow so shall you reap' so if you are being unjust with someone, it will come right back to you sooner or later.

When someone wrongs you, forgive him/ her as soon as you can. Talk to the other person if possible and try not to hold grudges because the pain only eats you up.

Fear can often cripple us, but try not to let it overpower your mind. You will learn to control your fears better and eventually let go of them with time as you work on the other Stoic principles.

Courage comes from within so to be courageous in life, you need to let go of your inner demons and work on overcoming your fears. This becomes easier when you learn to discipline yourself.

Self-discipline is the art of controlling your temptations and urges so you choose to do what is important instead of what is convenient and appealing.

All the different Stoic principles are inter-related; thus, as you work on all the rules one by one, you will then start to develop a well-rounded and virtuous personality. Let us move on to the next set of Stoic principles you need to work on to become stress-free, happy and peaceful.

The first lesson to be learned from Stoicism is the foundation of Stoicism – understanding your life's purpose and living life on purpose. If you don't know at the core what you want to do with your life, a thousand other things will rush in and take over. At the end of your life, you'll see that you lived other people's demands and interests rather than yours. You need to own your days so they do not own you. The first way to practice this is to start with a morning routine.

Morning Routine

The alarm goes off, and you have exactly one hour to be out your door. After you finally stop hitting the snooze button and spend a few minutes looking at your phone, you get up. You put together your coffee, feed pets, get your kids together, and help someone get something to eat. In ten minutes, the disorder of the a.m. urgency has taken over everything, in addition to that niggling feeling that you have some messages to send out before you head for that meeting at work. So much for easing into your day peacefully.

Even if you have a partner and use a tag team approach, it's still a major production to get into the shower and get ready for work. There are bags that need packed, homework to be gathered, bills to be paid, and goodbyes to be said as everyone goes out the front door.

Once you get to work, it's a dash to get things done before that morning meeting. Somehow, you wait for a quiet moment in order to pull together your final thoughts, to breathe or catch up, but that chance distances itself further and further. Later, you think maybe you can get some time at lunch, or after work, or at night, and then you're collapsing into bed only to wake up to the blaring alarm clock again.

That's the first scenario – the one where you don't have a morning routine. If you're like most people, this is you. However, let's look at how it CAN be.

The second scenario is the alarm goes off. This time, you have about two and a half hours. There's no snooze button during this scenario. Before anyone else in the household gets up, you get your ready-made coffee thanks to your pre-programmed coffee machine and slip into a remote area of the house where everything you need for your morning routine is set up. Your phone is upstairs because it's only there if you need it to wake you up. After you journal or read for a few minutes while you sip your coffee, you do a little meditation, yoga, or stretching to get ready for your morning workout. You enjoy the quiet surrounding you and focus on your movements. While you take some time afterward, you write out the main list for what you'll get done that day. After a shower, you're feeling peaceful and prepared to wake up the rest of the family and face the day.

Direct, or you're going to be put in a constant position of reacting.

While few people get to choose what happens during their day, the morning has the power to determine what or who is going to be leading the way and how much we give to our interests versus responding to someone else's as the day goes on. Your willpower is at its best in the morning, before you've had to fend off the slew of choices and issues that come your way. In other words, if you have a hard time keeping a commitment to yourself, you'll most likely be more successful making it part of the morning routine rather than holding off until later during the day.

From a psychological viewpoint, the morning hours offer some extra benefits. Exercising when you've fasted offers you greater benefits for insulin sensitivity and fat burning. There's the advantage of having that morning cortisol burst, too. This means extra energy that will go a long way in a morning exercise routine or to help you tackle your more challenging tasks. How many people postpone their exercise and responsibilities as long as possible, only to have to face them throughout the least active and driven hours in your day? By this point, it takes ten times the mental and physical capacity to make yourself follow through.

Another benefit is that you're more devoted to making healthier decisions during the day if you've already worked out in the morning, meditated, and performed other positive actions. You've previously invested in living a healthier lifestyle. You won't be subject to the troublesome sense of anxiety that follows you everywhere during the day. Your body is waiting to move and ready to protest at having to sit at a desk for eight hours.

People like to call their deferment of meditation and exercise as being self-discipline, but really, it's self-deprivation.

Developing a morning routine will let you assert your authority over the day. You take charge of your work-life equilibrium by paying yourself first, in a sense. Too many people do it the other way around and are left without enough time and energy to invest in themselves at the end of the day. As a result, many people feel they are at the mercy of their family and work demands. Responsibilities overwhelm them, and they end up getting stuck.

If you lead with your peace and well-being in the morning, however, you can get a lot more done during the day. Something essential will change when you start directing your day instead of responding to it. However you decide to design your morning routine, you're claiming the day before anyone or anything else is able to. Your actions, and the pattern of that action over time, will create a strong shift in your personal sense of fulfillment and happiness.

If you can't think of anything to start your day off with, let me help you.

Physical Health

The first thing people think of when they think of doing a physically healthy routine in the morning is exercise, but with that said, there are some other things that can help you physically in the morning. Make sure to go outside because the light can help you naturally wake up, and you'll feel more awake if you get in a good morning run or walk if it's outside. In addition, keep in mind that you don't have to move your whole workout routine to the morning if that doesn't work for you. Do a short stroll in the morning and save the rest for later. The idea is to do some kind of movement, like walking, yoga, or lifting a few weights, in addition to what else you feel would fuel your physical health for the day.

Mental Health

Your mind is just as important as the rest of your body. Yoga might do it for you, or a little time outside. Some people like to have their breakfast or coffee outside, and just that little action makes a huge difference for the day. Other people like to meditate from five to thirty minutes, and some like to read a book or write in a journal to center themselves. Others use the time to indulge in a little self-care.

Personal Vision

Your morning routine should have something that pertains to your personal vision. This is important because it relates to the direct-react problem in a larger way than just one day's agenda. Many of us have greater visualizations for our lives, such as things we want to try, careers we want to get into, hobbies we want to enjoy, or ideas they want to study, but they never do. If you're waiting until nine at night or a 'free' weekend, you can file that under the 'it's never going to happen' drawer.

Be brave, give a portion of your day's best energy to your vision, and maybe you'll learn a new hobby or get into a new career. Perhaps it's fitness, or it's a creative adventure. Maybe you want to network and build your portfolio to shift your career. Whatever it is, start your day off with it. If you stick with this one action every morning, you'll be amazed at your progress in just a few weeks, months, and over the time span of a year.

Do Something Productive

Like with any of the aforementioned ideas, this can mean something different for each person. Make a master list for your day, as a suggestion. You don't need to write down fifty things on a piece of paper. Just put down five of the most important ones, and make sure you do the most important and challenging ones first thing in the morning. Beyond this, you could do a chore that will make a difference in the following few days ahead. Devote a few hours to some financial planning or record keeping for the next week.

Experiment

Morning routines are YOUR time, so it should be time that is yours and involves no one else. Lock the door if you have to. So few people are accustomed to giving themselves this much-needed time. Putting yourself first during the morning can feel a little weird. You may be overwhelmed by how much you want to do in the morning, or you might not know how to fill the space. Just choose one thing at a time and build on the routine. If you stick with it and use it to benefit you, then you'll wonder how you ever lived without one.

Meditating on Your Life's Purpose

Start with one area of your life in mind. Choose an area where you're struggling or you want to experience a transformation, such as your career, your relationship with your spouse, or a hobby you want to turn into a business.

Begin to imagine the highest outcome you want to be living in from six to twelve months from this moment in this area of your life. Imagine living your life the way you want with all your hope and dreams coming true. What is the reality? Try not to get hung up on limitation or negativity.

Just let yourself get carried away with the wildest aspirations you can imagine.

Connect with a single goal you want to achieve in the following three months. If you choose a goal without a lot of meaning or weight, the end result is not going to feel that special. So be sure to choose something that's large enough that, once you achieve this goal, you'll feel accomplished and motivated to set another goal.

Now that you've connected with the goal, imagine your life once you've completed the goal. Make a mental movie or picture in your mind and step inside that visual representation.

Step outside of your image and imagine floating up above where you're at now, taking that mental image with you. Inhale deeply, and as you exhale, use your breath to energize that image, filling it with intention and positive energy. Do this a total of five times.

Imagine floating into the future and visualize dropping that internal representation of your goal down into your life at the date and time you set for when the goal should be completed.

Notice how the events between your current reality and future reality support you in realizing your objective.

Once you feel you've finished, return to reality, and as you keep your eyes closed, consider the action steps you need to take in the next week to move closer to the goal.

Breathe deeply in order to make yourself feel centered before you open your eyes. Jot down the list of action steps you need to take.

Keep your focus and take action. Each day, take an action step that gets you closer to achieving your goal.

In its most literal definition of the word, stoicism is an ancient philosophy born in Greece and Rome. But when people hear the word philosophy, often they think it's not for them or that it's impractical. In reality, stoicism is the most practical philosophy ever made. Entrepreneur Tim Ferriss says that it's a personal operating system for the mind. Stoicism is a fantastic operating system for thriving in high-stress environments. I think that's the main reason that people like Marcus Aurelius adopted stoicism. Even entrepreneurs, artists, and athletes today are still using stoicism 2,000 years later for one main reason: it can help you solve your problems.

In stoicism, there are three different disciplines. First of all, there is perception, or how you see things. Second of all, there's action - what you do about the things that you see. The third discipline is will, or how you bear and how you cope with the difficult things in life.

Stoicism, as mentioned, was founded in Athens by someone called Zeno of Citium. He was a merchant and in his life, he went through a horrible shipwreck. All of his belongings were taken away from him in his shipwreck. But through that process, he found philosophy and after him, there were three main famous stoics.

First, there was Marcus Aurelius, who was at the time the world's most powerful man, as he was the emperor of Rome and no man in the whole world was as powerful as him. Next was Epictetus, who was a slave and had an owner that would beat him. Then there was Seneca, who was a playwright. He was the most famous playwright in Rome, and he was also a political adviser. He was also one of the wealthiest men in the whole of Rome.

So you can see the diversity stoicism had, from absolute wealth, power, and riches to the complete opposite side of the spectrum—a slave who had nothing. It shows you that stoicism isn't like most philosophies, which are far removed from all of the inner workings of stoicism. It is a philosophy for the man or the woman in the workplace, the man or the woman competing in an athletic field, the philosophers, the politicians, the teachers, and everyone else in the world.

Stoicism is the philosophy for you, and it's the philosophy for me, because it acts as an inner compass that will help us make decisions day by day. It will help us have this sense of equanimity and a sense of being the best man or the best woman that we can be. Stoicism has a direct impact on every decision that we make and every decision that we think. It is being used to remove anxiety and depression and getting people to stop procrastinating, become disciplined, and start taking action. Stoicism is the best philosophy if you actually want to directly impact your brain and have it work in the most optimal way possible.

Physics and Logic

There are three main components of stoic philosophy, but the two most important will be discussed here briefly. The first is physics, which refers to the way the world works and all of its natural processes. The second is logic, which in essence is rational thought. The two aspects work in tandem to describe the way stoics view the world—through a lens of logic applied to reality.

Both physics and logic, even in the context of philosophy, can get a little complex, so only the basics will be covered here. Stoic physics gave stoics the ground to stand on, so to speak, by defining and exploring what the universe is made of and why it behaves the way it does. These explanations and observations could then be used to shed light on situations common to the human condition. Rather than life being one big enigma, stoics aimed to bring a little sense to the disorder.

Logic works with this by explaining the universe in ways that line up with reason. Stoic logic was extraordinarily similar to the logic that we know, teach, and use today, such as in computer programming. For example, if this, then this. Logics essentially explains what things are like and why they're not any other way by defining aspects of the world and statements as true and false.

The third aspect of the philosophy that we won't dive too deep into is ethics. Stoics through the ages have argued about where exactly ethics fits within the framework and what importance it holds, but the general view is that ethics cannot exist without logic, because logic can tell you what is ethical and what is not.

Irrational Passions

Irrational passions are what are known as voluntary responses, which as you can guess by the name are not positive aspects that stoics encourage. Irrational passions are also known as unhealthy or unnatural passions, indicating just how much the stoics felt they should be avoided. According to Zeno, unhappiness can be traced back to these irrational passions. There are many divisions and subdivisions of irrational passion, but what it all really boils down to is the following:

● Pain - envy, resentment, sorrow, anxiety, confusion

● Fear - shame, panic, shock, dread, superstition

● Craving - want, sexual desire, need for wealth and material possessions

● Pleasure - enchantment, spirited satisfaction

Stoics assert that these irrational passions lead to unhappiness. You might be uncertain as to why pleasure is on this list, but stoics believe that an excess of many things, including pleasure, is detrimental. Excess pleasure can cause us to forsake logic, which is a big no-no in stoicism.

Good Passions

Just as there are irrational passions, there is another side of the coin, the good passions. These are, you guessed it, the ones you want. These good passions aren't virtues, per se, but they contribute to our happiness and our ability to live virtuously. Keep in mind that the main thing separating the good passions from the irrational is that good passions stem from a place of reason. There is logic behind their existence, which makes them natural while the irrational passions are unnatural.

Good passions can be described as follows:

● Joy or delight (in place of pleasure)

● Caution or discretion (in place of fear)

● Wishing or willing (in place of craving)

All of these passions come from a place of logic and reason. Joy is a logical feeling stemming from something positive, caution is logical and necessary for self-preservation, and wishing is a natural human quality that is also logical, because wishing and/or willing is how to discover what's important to us.

One aspect of Stoicism is an idea that ethics is centered on the effort. The study of ethics is supported by physics and logic. These make up the topoi of Stoicism.

We are going to look at each one, but we must understand how they connect. Stoicism is a practical philosophy that is meant to help people live their lives practicing virtues. During the Roman period, the emphasis moved to achieving apatheia. This was only possible by practicing the topos of ethics.

This was supported by studying logic and physics. Logic roughly means studying how to reason about the world. Physics meant studying the world.

Both of these, physics and logic are related to ethics. Any time a Stoic talks about a soul or God, they are referring to a physical entity that can be identified by the principle of the universe. This is what makes humanity possible. Stoics would use imagery to show others the relationship between ethics, physics, and logic. The most famous simile is an egg. The shell was logic, the white was ethics, and the yellow was physics. But, seeing as how they are supposed to relate to one another, this is rather misleading. They possibly misunderstood the biology of eggs. Physics should nurture ethics. This means the first should have been the white and the last the yellow. The first example that comes to mind is that of a garden: the fence would be logical because it defends the inside and defines the boundaries. The soil is the physics, since it gives nutrients power by understanding the world. That leaves the fruits as ethics. This is the objective of Stoicism.

Stoics disagreed on the order in which these need to be taught. The main point is a natural philosophy is where you can't find a distinction between should and what is. This is expected in moral philosophy since what a person should do (ethics) is informed by the person's knowledge of how the world works (physics) and their capacity to reason these things correctly (logic).

Let's take a closer look at logic. Stoics made early contributions about the importance of logic proper and epistemology. A lot has been written about it. Stoics believed that a Sage could achieve perfect knowledge; they actually relied on an actual cognitive and moral progress since physics and logic are related to and function to serve ethics. They called this making progress. They had an ongoing dispute about Academic Skeptics.

Stoics didn't maintain that everything was true but that some things were cataleptic, or would lead to comprehension and others weren't. The cataleptic is what comes from something in existence and is according to the thing and what has been imprinted and stamped. The non-cataleptic could come from anything that doesn't exist or, if it does exist, then it isn't in accordance with the thing, and it isn't either distinct or clear.

The Stoics do admit that a person's perception might be wrong, like with dreams or hallucinations. With proper training, it lets one make progress with figuring out cataleptic from non-cataleptic impressions. It is possible to absorb many impressions since impressions will lead to forming concepts and making progress. The Stoics relied on what modern people would call inference. The best explanation was their conclusion that skin has holes due to the fact that we sweat.

Cataleptic impressions are not known. The Stoics made distinctions between false or weak opinions, apprehension, and knowledge. Allowing assent to an impression is the first step to knowledge, but is more stable and structured than anyone's impression could ever be. In this sense, they held a coherentist view of justification, and like all the ancients, a correspondence of truth.

When talking about logic that is closest to what we conceive, Stoics made a huge contribution. Their system of logic saw that all arguments are rationale and differ since they have a lot in common with today's logic. To put it simply, Stoic philosophy was created with five logics; they satisfied four rules to be used in arguments that were used to bring philosophy to the basics.

The larger approach was characterized as propositional logic. Stoics showed the difference between assertive and sayables. The latter is broad and covers curses, invocations, oaths, imperatives, and questions. The assertibles are sayables that are used to create statements. Look at this example, "If Johnny lives in Texas then Johnny lives in America." This is a conditional composite assertible that is made from the assertibles that Johnny lives in Texas and Johnny lives in America. The difference between assertibles and propositions is that falsehood or truth could change in time. Johnny lives in Texas is true for now. It might not be tomorrow, it is possible that it might be true again next month. The falsehood or truth is an assertible, and the fact of being false or true is a necessary condition for being assertible.

Stoics were worried about how valid the arguments were and not the logic of the truths. This is understandable with their interest in using logic to guard their gardens. They introduced modality to their logic. The most important properties are probability, plausibility, impossibility, necessity, non-possibility, and possibility. This approach was practical and modern since it gave attention toward the assertibles because they will give agreement even if they are false. Some assertibles could be true.

Let's move on to physics. This includes what we call theology, metaphysics, and natural science.

When talking about cosmology and natural science, Stoics tried to live with nature.

This tells us to make the best efforts in understanding nature. The modern view is different than this one: this study isn't ending, but an accessory that will show us how to live.

Stoics believed that everything in existence is corporeal, including soul and God. They recognized categories such as sayables, time, and void. This might look like it contradicts itself, but it isn't any different than modern philosophical naturalists that say a person can talk about abstract concepts that are grounded in materialistic things since they are being thought about by beings like ourselves.

They embraced a vital understanding of nature that was ingrained in two principles: one was active like God and reason; the other was passive like matter and substance. The active one is indestructible. The passive one is classified by the elements of air, earth, fire, and water and can be destroyed and recreated for eternity. The cosmos is a living being, and it is identified with fire. Consequently,

God is imminent and is identified with the cosmic fire. The Stoics don't recognize the concept of a prime person outside space and time because something incorporeal can't act since it doesn't have more powers.

Cosmic conflagrations will repeat themselves exactly the same way since Nature/God has everything laid out the best way possible and there isn't any reason to change. According to Eusebius during the cosmic conflagration, the seed possesses everything and is the reason everything has happened, is happening, or will happen. It is the interweaving and ordering of things that we know as fate, truth, knowledge, and inevitable law of everything that exists.

Metaphysically, Stoics were very determined people. They believed that when the circumstances surrounding the cause and the cause are the same, then things should turn out a certain way. They did believe in chance but thought it was a measure of ignorance: random events are just events that humans can't understand.

The Stoics' ethics are clear. They get explained by Cicero. Try to aim for the place between what we call incompatibilism and libertarianism. Stoics shifted their emphasis from responsibility to dignity and worth.

Regarding ontology, Stoics were anti-corpuscularian because atoms breached the concept of unity within the cosmos. It might be tempting to look at this like quantum physics and see the universe was constructed from a wave function but this would be anachronistic.

Ethics isn't just a subject. It is a practical one. Later Stoics believed that ethics was how we are supposed to live. It wasn't an easy task. Some things we can control, others we can't.

Early Stoics were more theoretical with their approach. They attempted to systematize and defend their doctrines from critics. The early Stoic motto was, follow nature. They meant both rational-providential aspect and human nature. They thought that since they were social animals, they could bring rational judgment to deal with problems that arose in a person's life. The idea of following nature was closely related to the concept of appropriation. For Stoics, people have natural tendencies that morally develop. Tendencies start as instincts and then refine as we age and beyond. It's interesting to see that all the accounts of the beginnings of moral behavior are compatible with the findings with both cognitive and evolutionary science.

So behave in a way to advance our goals and interests. We identify with other's interests. We find ways to move through life's fluctuations. Stoics relate these properties to four virtues of wisdom, justice, courage, and temperance. We need courage and temperance to reach goals we have set for ourselves. Justice extends from our concern over our close friends. Wisdom lets us deal with what happens.

This leads us to how these virtues relate to each other. To start, Stoics recognized the four virtues but saw more specific ones within each category. Wisdom includes resourcefulness, discretion, and good judgment. Temperance can be divided into self-control, sense of honor, and propriety. Courage can be divided down into magnanimity, confidence, and perseverance. Justice is broken into sociability, kindness, and piety. Their virtue was more unitary than what might be found on this kind of list. Justice is thought of as wisdom and applied to everyday living. Courage with the help of wisdom will help with endurance. Wisdom, with the help of temperance, helps in making the right choices. This can be further elaborated with pluralism in an underlying unity, making them inseparable, so one can't be courageous and intemperate.

Some have drawn parallels between these virtues, the topoi, and what are called the three disciplines: assent, action, and desire. Desire has been called acceptance. It comes from studying physics, most importantly, the belief of cause and effect within the universe. It asks one to train themselves to want the things universe will allow and not the things it doesn't. A good metaphor to use as an example is taking a dog for a walk on a leash. The dog can decide to walk with its owner and have a good time or fight each step and take the risk of getting hurt. This is called loving your fate or enduring what the universe gives you. Desire is linked to courage to allow you to follow the cosmos. It is also linked to temperance so you can control your desires.

Action, also known as philanthropy, is prosocial. The basic principle is that humans need to develop a concern for others. It is connected closest to justice. The most famous quote comes from Marcus Aurelius: "Men exist for the sake of one another. Teach them then to bear with them." You can see an example of philanthropy in the first sentence. The second shows that the emperor's duty was to engage others or try to deal with their bad behavior.

Assent refers to mindfulness. Don't confuse this with the type of mindfulness that Buddhists practice. This discipline is necessary to help us decide what we need to reject or accept while walking through this world, or more specifically, how to make the right judgment. It can be linked to practical wisdom and logic.

Ethics concerns itself exclusively with virtue. The Stoics believed that several things are needed for a harmonious life. These include education, health, and wealth.

Stoics balance their world by introducing the concept of being indifferent. We must distinguish between what has value and what doesn't. The things that have a value to us would be things like education, wealth, and health. The things that don't have any value are things like ignorance, poverty, and sickness. This is a brilliant concept since you basically get the best of both worlds. People will seek to be a person with moral integrity, trying to achieve harmony without thinking about material problems.

The Stoics believed by studying logic and physics it could change the way we know ethics. The nature of the universe is what they believed in. If they only accepted the latter view, could they still pursue happiness? The preferred answer is no.

Some have argued that the theocratic principle affects how people look at the relationship between virtue and the cosmos. This doesn't change virtue's content or affect how one conceives happiness. This is due to the fact that physics inform ethics. It does this in an underdetermined way so that ethics isn't independent of physics and therefore can't be read off it. Ethics is natural but it doesn't erase the ought/is divide.

The ancient Stoics believed there was a physical God. They equated this to the cosmos being organized and getting distributed along the universe. They thought that understanding the cosmos would help them understand ethics and would help them live their lives. Their metaphysics underdetermined their conception of their ethics and allowed them to believe in a godly position that was created to deal with all the criticism they were getting from the atomists.

It has become clear to me through my own experience and in my work with all levels of performers, that what really stops people from doing what they already know how to do is their failure to recognize the impact emotions have on their actions and performance. This becomes apparent when they can't apply their everyday skills and knowledge under challenging or stressful situations. The best of the best recognize the importance of this emotional intelligence, not only in realizing their potential but in sustaining it over time.

What are emotions? Emotions are nothing but feelings or a state of mind, where your conscious focus generated a certain mental and physical state. The way we feel is arguably the most important aspect of life. No matter what we want, whether it be more money, better relationships, more time or a better body, it all comes down to emotions. Huh? Yes! See it is not a better body or more money you are really after but rather the feelings you associate to having more money or a better body. Emotions form the core of our lives and more specifically the human emotions that drive our behavior. Everything we do in our lives we do either out of our need to avoid pain or our need to gain pleasure. All the emotions we experience are not only rooted in our own minds, but they are even "created" by us. Some people think that the emotions they experience are entirely out of their control, and that emotions are spontaneous reactions to the events of our lives. The truth is that suppressing or ignoring an emotion will only amplify it until you deal with it. If we heed and utilize the signals that emotions give us we can change the quality of our lives and experience of life immediately. All emotions serve a purpose and a very important purpose as such. Don't feel bad about not knowing about this or how important it is to you. We all follow similar paths in our lives. The first and most important thing in our lives is school. We are exhorted to study hard, learn as much as we can and perform as good as possible. Technical skills are the focus of our education and we are measured according to how much we know. There is no systematic approach to teach us how to handle ourselves under pressure, how to become self-aware, and how to create consistent, sustainable relationships. These things simply are not part of the curriculum. It is left up to us to develop these skills on our own in the schoolyard, on the playing field, at the office and at home.

The ability to manage our emotions effectively may be more significant at this time in history than ever before. We live in a world where environments are being damaged beyond foreseeable repair, whole countries are on the verge of bankruptcy, never mind the millions of individuals without jobs and with homes in foreclosure, and as a result, there is a growing divide between the 'haves' and the 'have nots'. "Us and them" attitudes continuously permeate our planet, creating tensions that are ending daily in thousands of examples of emotional hijacking and emotionally charged actions; acts of stupidity or levels of violence, perpetrated by often desperate human beings, consequences of people made to feel increasingly stressed, unsafe, overwhelmed and threatened. Believe it or not, emotions drive our behavior and the way we interact with each other and perform in our lives. Behind every word, action or deed are beliefs, perceptions, reasoning and thoughts, thoughts that are only as powerful as the emotions that carry them. Who hasn't felt a sudden rush of anger, so strong it becomes un-controllable and we find ourselves saying or doing something that we later deeply regret. Or experienced a sudden wave of sadness for no apparent reason, giving rise to a train of thoughts that in turn fills us with self-pity and often lingering depression. It isn't a good feeling. Just a niggling feeling of anxiety and worry in the back of our minds, when no amount of encouraging remarks from loved ones such as "don't worry!" can change our perception that worrying is just what we are meant to be doing. Emotions drive our perceptions and what we think because they are stronger and more powerful than our cognitive ability for reasoning. More often than not, we aren't even consciously aware of the emotions in our body that our driving our thought process. When we become aware of our emotions, we label them and they become feelings, giving us the consciousness to begin the process of emotional self-regulation, if we so choose. For example, when I become aware that my emotions are unsettling and that I am in fact feeling anxious, I become further aware that this anxiety might cause me to overreact at other smaller things. Once you realize that you are in a state of despair and anxiety, then you can begin to shift yourself in a different state of mind.

You can begin the process of managing your feelings so that they no longer have a stressful impact. I can remove myself for a few minutes, do some breathing exercises and take charge of my internal emotional state, changing it to one that gives me some clarity of thought, whereas, I can plan and write down a few steps that I may take to address whatever is causing the anxiety, or at least gain some insight into how

I can better handle myself. I can then go to my situation with a renewed sensitivity and even mindfulness of their needs as well as my own.

Consciousness and self-awareness allow us to take charge of our emotional state, enhancing our ability to become sensitive to our own needs, the needs of the collective whole in any given situation. The power of such consciousness is in the intention of using it to manage the impact we have on one another, to maintain a lasting awareness of the absolute power of emotions, that they underlie everything, and to take responsibility for that personal power, each of us individually. As Aldous Huxley famously said;

Four courses from antiquity on self-discipline

Stoicism is an early philosophy. The perfect for the stoic would be to reveal equanimity. Stoicism's four virtues are temperance, justice, courage, and wisdom. Temperance is subdivided to subject self-control and modesty. I believe that with the subject, everything else falls into place. Discipline is philosophy, mindset, and the action that keeps you towards anything person is pursuing, in a regular and making progress. Stoicism cultivates. Listed below are four classes I have removed that have helped me built a subject in regards to my own health and wellbeing?

1. Find wise people to emulate

With no ruler to take action, you cannot make jagged straight. We will need to recognize the significance of getting. These characters serve to emulate. Pick and select somebody who's currently living a life that is fantastic. By life, that is great. I mean, imagine the individual locate and that you would like to become. Listen to what they say, learn from them, and what's more, to what they do not do listen. Humble yourself and adopt ignorance. Stick to Socrates' words and acknowledge positively to yourself, then you understand that you understand nothing. What's motivating this individual's activities, their aspirations are the impacts they experience occurring to them. Changing your mindset will build confidence and confidence in yourself be and keep on course. This understanding of you and your life will be rewarded.

2. Review your day

It is not enough to go to sleep without even contemplating the classes' consequences and knowledge that you obtained during the day. It is a shame. Considering thinking at night was known as 'day retrospections.' One can predict this journaling now.

Request yourself,

• Now, what exactly did I do?

• Where was my discipline, and where did I do well?

• What did I do evil? Why did this happen? How do I improve?

Among the finest ways would be to scrutinize yourself, find your weak spots. Be honest and utilize this opportunity. Practicing to a constant basis will make it possible for you to become through every single step of your day as you'll be collecting information articulate and to formulate responses to the queries that are later.

3. Your distractions are your own doing

Marcus Aurelius said,

"If you're distressed by anything external, the pain isn't on account of the item itself, but to your own estimate of it and this, you have the ability to revoke at any time." Getting upset, being bothered by things that are little is terrible for the subject. You've got a goal, you are working and then distress and ideas about something [out of your hands] de-rail you. It's to use Epictetus' dichotomy of management. Reinforce to yourself what's outside of your hands and what's inside your control; should you take it and adopt what's outside of your hands, you may experience tranquility.

Refer to the following wording next time you are upset and distracted:

• have you got a problem in your lifetime?

• No? Then do not worry.

• Yes? Would you do something about it?

• Yes? Then do not worry.

• No? Then do not worry.

As soon as you find something that derailed your pursuits, comprehends it, does not ignore it. Never strive never to make a mistake going and regret your words or actions.

134

4. Every day is a new life

Seneca stated,

"Begin at once to dwell and count each separate day as a separate life."

A day does not have to become a week; a week does not need to develop into a year. The instant that you wake up does not forget that the day is a brand new life. The last should not be forgotten; however, it shouldn't be. All actions from prior days should be pondered on a function no besides to haul you down and are out of your hands. Publish the anchor and move by focusing and opening your eyes. It doesn't mean that you've failed, and there's no use in continuing if you binged in your daily diet. This would not define your personality if you did not work out when you know that you ought to have. Your capacity is exactly what frees you to a powerful and disciplined individual.

When it comes to self-development, a lot has been said about how important it is to be able to experience self-control and to be resilient. Naturally, these are two incredibly important abilities to have in life.

If one is unable to control themselves, it is going to be a challenge for them to achieve anything worthwhile. Instead, they will most likely get caught up in endless distractions and trivialities.

An Analogy

One way to understand what can take place, if someone has no control, can be to imagine a child in a toy shop. In one moment they will be drawn to one area and, in the blink of an eye, they will be drawn to another area.

This child won't be able to stick to any one area, which will stop them from getting an

understanding of anything. The reason being is that as soon as they start to concentrate on one toy, they will end up seeing another toy and soon end up walking   away.
A Wasted life

To behave in this way as an adult is going to stop one from being able to stick to anything. Just like a child in a toy shop, they can start something and then put it to one side shortly after.

There can the impact this will have on their career, along with other areas of their life. For example, if one can control themselves, it is most likely going to be a challenge for them to eat sensibly and to exercise on a regular basis.

Where has it all gone?

One could then look back on their life and wonder what they have been doing; it may seem as though life has just passed them by. Their emotions and their thoughts will then have controlled them, as opposed to one being able to manage these parts of their being.

Without the ability to keep their thoughts and feelings in check, it will have had a negative effect on their life. One will be like a small boat that is tossed around the ocean, not a big ship that can handle just about anything.

The Other Part

And if one is unable to keep going during the setbacks that arise, it is also unlikely that they will be able to achieve anything that is significant. As soon as things heat up, so to speak, they will drop out.

They might be fairly big built or they might not, but what they won't have is the inner muscle that will enable them to keep going. Someone like this will want an easy like, not the strength to handle the challenges that life brings.

An another Analogy

This will be like going to a gym and not wanting to lift anything that is too heavy.

This will make it easier for them to lift things, yet what it won't do is allow someone to become stronger.

It could then be said that they will be wasting their time, and that it might have been better if they had stayed at home. Taking this into account, the having the ability to tolerate pain is clearly vital.

The Dark Side

However, while being stoic is going to allow one to handle life, it can have a negative effect if it is taken to the extreme. Or to be more precise, this can be something that takes place due to someone's interpretation of what it means to be stoic.

Through reading up about it, someone can believe that they need to deny how they feel and to basically dominate their emotions. Their mind is then going to be in a constant battle with their body.

One Dimensional

Being this way may allow them to move forward and to achieve their goals, but it can also set them up to have problems when it comes to connecting with others. Their emotions, the things that will allow them to connect to others and for others to connect to them, will be pushed down.

They are then going to be human, but they might come across as though they don't really feel anything. This can then set them up to have a very lonely existence, and what they achieve probably won't fill this gap.

A Deeper Look

What someone like this may find is that they didn't have a good relationship with their emotions to begin with, with this being the reason why they were drawn to stoicism. Or why they came to believe that behaving in this way was what it meant to be stoic.

One could then continue to deny how they feel and believe that they were doing the right thing. This would have provided them with validation that they needed to keep the truth at bay: that they are avoiding how they feel.

Way Back

This can show that they are carrying a lot of pain due to what took place during their early years. Perhaps this was a time when they didn't receive the care that they needed in order to develop a healthy relationship with their emotions.

At this time in their life, pushing their emotions down would have been a way for them to handle the pain they were in. As a result of what they experienced, it would have also most likely given them the ability to be able to handle a fair amount of pain.

Awareness

If one had an early childhood where they had to disconnect from their emotions and had no other choice than to tolerate extreme pain, it is not going to be a surprise if they are drawn to 'stoicism'. This form of stoicism is then simply going to be another defence that one will use to avoid their inner wounds.

If one can relate to this, and they want to become an integrated human being, they may need to reach out for external support. This is something that can be provided by the assistance of a therapist or a healer, for instance.

LIFE'S HARDSHIPS can be incredibly painful, and if you lack the necessary qualities to get through hardships, they can be even more challenging for you to embrace. Learning how to deal with life's hardships through resilience, confidence, and calmness can be a powerful opportunity for you to overcome hardships in a more peaceful and effective manner. Through this, you can start to truly see the benefit of Stoicism in your life as you begin to see yourself peacefully and confidently navigating the many challenges that life has to offer. While you may not always swiftly move through each hardship with grace and strength, if you can even begin to improve your ability to navigate these hardships, you will find yourself in a better place. Remember, the goal is always to improve and to try to offset what you can, not to become perfect in any way.

Your Judgment Harms You Most

Anytime you find yourself amidst a hardship, it is crucial for you to slow down and assess your judgment. Your judgment over a situation is what will help you decide what it means to you, as well as how to respond to that situation. It is imperative that you learn how to overcome the knee-jerk reaction of going with your initial judgment and take the time to honestly assess each and every single situation you come across. The more you can step back and understand the situation, the easier it will be for you to see it clearly and honestly, and address it in a Stoic, level-headed manner.

Your judgment, above all else, has the capacity to harm you the most. When you choose to go with your knee-jerk judgment, you often find yourself obsessing over a judgment that is not necessarily true but rather is rooted in your emotional triggers. For example, let's say someone has not talked to you in a few days. You might initially think that it is because this person does not like you, which creates a judgment that promotes low self-confidence, a lack of peace, stress, and overwhelm inside of you. You may start racking your mind to discover what you did wrong or how you may have upset this person enough that they did not want to talk to you. In reality, they may have simply been busy and, therefore, not had time to connect with you for a few days, and they will likely tell you all about it when they contact you.

It is best that you never assume how another person is feeling or what another person is thinking, no matter how well you may think you know them. While you can certainly use empathy and compassion to help you gain some perspective, assuming that you know exactly what someone is thinking or feeling can result in you becoming close-minded to the truth. It can also result in you acting on assumptions before you have the real answer, leaving you wasting energy on worrying thoughts and feelings that were ultimately unnecessary.

Even if someone is angry with you or you are in conflict with another person or situation, it is not helpful for you to carry judgments that create more harm for you. Rather than creating judgments that encourage you to hold onto contempt, hatred, anger, frustration, sadness, or other difficult emotions toward that person, choose a judgment that helps you overcome these feelings. Resolution-based judgments will support you in creating resolutions in your life, thus providing you with the answers and closure that you need from every difficult situation you face.

Confidence and Calmness Trump Anger

Anger is an emotion that holds great value, though it can also hold great power. For many, they never properly learn how to embrace and use this power effectively, and so they end up being destroyed by it. It is not uncommon for people to say things out of anger or to behave in ways that are fueled by anger, only to later regret what they have said or done.

Unchecked anger can lead to expressions that feel as though they are beyond your control, even though it is up to you to take responsibility for them in the end. Rather than feeling controlled by your emotions and being left to take responsibility for things you are guilty of or ashamed for, you need to learn how to control your anger and channel its power for a positive purpose.

Anger is, essentially, an emotion that lets you know that you feel as though you have been violated in a way. Generally, this means one of your boundaries have been crossed, and you feel as though you have to defend yourself and protect yourself in order to avoid having this violation hurt you in some way. Understanding the root cause of anger will not help you avoid feeling anger in the future, but it can help you begin to express anger in a healthier and more intentional way.

Choosing to express your anger with confidence and calmness means that you are choosing to acknowledge that you are angry and that you are going to assert yourself in a way that is not uncontrollable. For example, rather than lashing out or getting into a screaming match with someone, you are going to politely ask for some space, identify what boundary has been crossed, and then find a resolution to help you fix that scenario. You can then use your anger to give you the confidence you need to assert the boundary in any way that you see fit. This could include letting the person know it exists and explaining that you wish it not to be crossed again, or it could be putting space between yourself and that person or even terminating your relationship with them if they routinely cross your boundaries and show no remorse. Ultimately, you get to decide what the answer is going to be. However, it is best that you make it after the initial burst of anger, and then use that burst of anger to give you the energy you need to see that resolution through. This way, anger is a productive and helpful emotion for you, and it supports you in getting through your

148

hardships faster and in a way that represents a greater sense of strength and integrity for you.

Your Expectations Are to Blame

When we find ourselves facing hardships, it is important that we always do our best to take responsibility for the hardships that we are in. Since we can only control our judgment and our voluntary actions, it stands to reason that there must be something we can do within our judgment and voluntary actions to support ourselves in overcoming hardships.

Expectations are a big one when it comes to hardship, as often we find ourselves in conflict or feeling let down because we have had expectations that went unmet. For example, in a relationship, you may be angry with your partner because you expected they would behave in a certain way or say a specific thing, and they didn't. At work, you may be feeling let down because you expected that you were going to be the one to get a raise and a promotion, but instead, it was awarded to your colleague. Online, you may feel let down because you expected people would like a new picture or status you posted more than they did, and yet you only got a few likes or no likes at all.

We have a tendency to create expectations and then to assign specific meanings and values to the expectations we create. As a result, we find ourselves attached to our expectations and left feeling deeply let down when our expectations go unmet. If you want to change this cycle and stop attracting so much hardship in your life, you need to change your expectations. There is a common saying that goes, "expect the worst and hope for the best." This saying is actually incredibly valuable in that it reminds you that anything can happen, including the worst thing, and that you should expect that it will. In doing so, you mentally prepare yourself for anything that could happen. By keeping yourself in a state of hoping for the best, though, you ensure that you stay open for positive things to happen so that you do not end up pessimistic as a result of always expecting the worst to happen.

Life Is Supposed to Be Challenging

The American dream sells this idea that you should be able to have a happy family that never faces challenges, an abundance of cash and resources to supply your lifestyle, and everything you could ever want in life. This dream is promoted through popular culture by way of music, movies, advertisements, and many other mainstream things that sell this vision of always being happy and fulfilled to our society.

The truth is, life is not meant to be easy all the time. As strange as it sounds, if you never knew hardship, you would never know fulfillment because you would never know what it would be like to be without struggling or suffering. By that breath, we can conclude that life is supposed to be challenging. It is in the challenges, specifically in the way that you respond to such challenges, that you gain the opportunity to learn, grow, and improve the overall quality of your life. Rather than wishing challenges away, welcome them when they come and recognize that they are an inevitable part of your life. Then, see if you can identify what you can learn or practice during these challenges so that you can endure them with greater resilience, confidence, and calmness. Once you have completed the challenge, express gratitude, and move on to the next thing in your life.

Focus on Your Present Experience

When we are amidst hardships, it can be easy to quickly predict doom for our future. You might find yourself automatically assuming that this hardship will be long-lasting, will have a great impact on your life, and will ruin everything. This all-or-nothing sense of doom is common when we are facing troubles because we find ourselves attempting to mentally prepare for the longevity of the trouble we are facing. Of course, no one can predict how long something is going to happen for, or what is going to happen as a result of any given event that you experience. For that reason, stressing too much about the future of a troubling situation is not worth your time. Often, the outcome will be different from that which you stressed about anyway, meaning all that time you spent stressing in an effort to prepare yourself was a waste.

Be mindful of what could happen in the future, but otherwise keep yourself focused on the present moment. Look for ways that you can navigate your hardship now and for things that you can do to help yourself experience resolve now. Make your choices for resolutions based on your best-educated guess on how they will work out, and then commit to seeing them through. If, after some time, you find they are not working, or more information has been revealed to you, you discover that this resolution no longer fits, then you can change it. In the meantime, always try to stay present during a challenging moment so that you can do the best you can to see that challenge all the way through.

Always Be a Student of Life

Challenges can make it feel hard for you to step back and assess the situation from afar. It is not uncommon for you to become so emotionally wrapped up in a hardship that you struggle to see it from any perspective other than your own. Still, taking a moment to step back and see your hardships from different perspectives can go a long way in helping you learn and grow as a person.

When you step back and look at your hardships from a different perspective, you gain the ability to understand them to a deeper level. Through this, you gain the capacity to understand how all of your actions may have contributed to the hardship, and possibly locate patterns of behaviors that you tend to repeat under certain circumstances. You also gain the ability to better understand other people and how they play into the circumstance, and more about the situation itself. This wisdom can support you in deepening your ability to navigate future hardships more effectively, while also having greater control over your emotions and your mindset.

CHAPTER 14: HOW TO FIND PEACE WITHIN YOURSELF

"The mind that is free from passions is a citadel, for man has nothing more secure to which he can fly for refuge and repel every attack."

---Marcus Aurelius

Finding peace with ourselves no matter what the outside world thinks of us

To the Stoics, peace does not depend on external things. In fact, no matter what the external circumstances may be, peace can be achieved. That is why, do not bother about what the outside world thinks or says about you. As put by Marcus Aurelius, "You shouldn't give circumstances the power to rouse anger, for they don't care at all." He also wrote, "If you are distressed by anything external, the pain is not due to the thing itself, but to your estimate of it; and this you have the power to revoke at any moment."

156

The outside world such as how people act or think is outside your control. If you allow other people to direct your path, then it would be impossible for you to find peace. You can find wisdom in the words of Epictetus: "Happiness and freedom begin with a clear understanding of one principle: Some things are within our control, and some things are not. It is only after you have faced up to this fundamental rule and learned to distinguish between what you can and can't control that inner tranquility and outer effectiveness become possible." Realize this, and inner peace will be well within your reach. One of the reasons why people fail to do this is because they do not accept the fact that they cannot control the outside world. Another reason is that they bother too much about what other people might think of them. The problem here is that if you do not let go of such worries, then it would be impossible for you to let go and find peace.

Here is another enlightening teaching by another Stoic named Gaius Musonius Rufus: "In our control is the most beautiful and important thing, the thing because of which even the god himself is happy--- namely, the proper use of our impressions ... we must concern ourselves absolutely with the things that are under our control and entrust the things not in our control to the universe."

Peace of mind

According to Epictetus, "Man is not worried by real problems so much as by his imagined anxieties about real problems." This is a wise teaching. If you come to think of it, is not that the thoughts that you have in your mind are actually the ones that are giving you stress? If you want to minimize stress and have a more peaceful mindset, then you should take control of your thoughts. Stop worrying too much. According to Science, your thoughts also have a major influence on your health and mood. Hence, it would really be helpful if you take the effort to master your thoughts and think of more positive things. As put by Epictetus, "As you think, so you become. Avoid superstitiously investing events with power or meanings they don't have. Keep your head. Our busy minds are forever jumping to conclusions, manufacturing and interpreting signs that aren't there. Assume, instead, that everything that happens to you does so for some good. That if you decided to be lucky, you are lucky. All events contain an advantage for you- if you look for it."

It is worth noting that even if you read all the books ever written, it will not give you peace of mind. The only way to achieve it is by working on it. This may take time, so start working on it as early as possible. That is why you should start today. Make it a point to develop your peace of mind. A good start is by not entertaining negative thoughts that cross your mind. Instead, think of positive thoughts. Of course, this does not mean that you should be blind to facing problems, but you need to limit your exposure to stressful situations. A good way to do this is by giving just enough time to think about your problems. After which you should only entertain positive thoughts. Take note, however, that this may take time to master. The mind is simply hard to control. It will bombard you with lots of seemingly important thoughts. However, if you persist and practice enough, you will soon be able to tame the mind and achieve peace of mind.

Another way to achieve peace of mind is by practicing meditation. Even a simple breathing meditation can do wonders.

Exercise: Relaxing Meditation

Sit or lie down. The important thing to note is to keep your spine straight, but not tense.

You may close your eyes if you want.

Take five deep breaths. Focus on breathing.

Become aware of your body. Relax even deeply.

Let your thoughts come and go. Do not force them and do not focus your attention on them.

After five to ten minutes you can stop, however feel free to continue.

That is it. As you can see, the breathing meditation is very simple, just like many other meditation techniques. Now, if you have not meditated before, you may think that the instructions seem too simple and could not help you in achieving peace of mind. But, if you just give it a try and continue to practice it regularly, you will feel and realize just how wonderful this meditation is. Of course, you are also free to try other meditation techniques. It is worth noting that many meditators practice this simple breathing meditation for many years.

When you practice meditation, you will notice that it is not that simple to focus on your breath. While focusing on the breath, you will notice that you get bombarded with so many thoughts. In Buddhism, this is called as the monkey mind where the mind is like a monkey that jumps from one branch (thought) to another continuously. However, with continuous practice, there will be fewer thoughts that will bother you and you will be more able to quiet your mind. Within a few days of practicing meditation, you will already begin to feel its remarkable benefits.

Now, you might be thinking: Can peace of mind be achieved even when everything around you is in chaos? The answer is yes. Do not forget that Stoicism was made during the time when the world was falling apart with kingdoms waging war against one another.

Here is another teaching from Marcus Aurelius: "Today I escaped from anxiety. Or no, I discarded it, because it was within me, in my own perceptions---not outside." There are so many people out there who are so anxious. They have stressful thoughts. Although they may have a reason for having such thoughts, if only they are able to let them go, then they would realize that their problem is a lot less serious than they think. It is your perception of things that can make a big difference.

Realize the truth that peace is within you. You only need to look within and recognize it. Control what you can and let go of those that are outside of your control.

Practical exercises and meditations

Here are some more exercises and technics that you can try. After all, the only way to really learn and appreciate the meaning of Stoicism is to live its teachings.

Technic #1

Discipline of assent

The discipline of assent is a Stoic practice of not giving in to strong impulses. As put by Epictetus, "Hold on a moment; let me see who you are and what you represent. Let me put you to the test." So, how do you apply this teaching? Well, this is something that you can use in your daily life. Pay attention to situations that provoke a strong impulse. This can be in the form of anger, sadness, or even lust. Just before you make an action, you should postpone it for a while and view the situation as if it is not a part of you --- which is, in fact, the truth. You will see that simply by postponing your reaction, you will be more able to handle the situation more calmly and effectively. This is why the discipline of assent is considered an important practice in Stoicism, especially when it comes to improving self-control.

Tip:

Do not be discouraged if you fail to control yourself from the strong impulse. Just keep on trying. This exercise will definitely improve your character. By separating yourself from the emotion or situation, you will be more able to take appropriate actions.

Technic #2

Self-denial

Stoics also practice self-denial from time to time. So, how do you do it? Simply deny yourself some pleasure. For example, if you like to smoke five cigarettes in a day, then only smoke two sticks today. According to the Stoics, by practicing self-denial, you will be more able to appreciate the beauty of something. Of course, this does not just apply to smoking, but also to other more important things in life. In a study made at Stanford Institute, it was also found that by practicing self-denial, you will be able to develop your willpower to a significant degree.

Tip:

When you practice this technique, be sure that you deny yourself of something that gives you pleasure or something that you like. For example, if you like having a big meal, then maybe you can try to skip lunch or just eat a smaller serving. Do not forget that the main objective of this exercise is not to make you suffer, but to teach you to realize and appreciate things (and people) more fully.

Technic #3

Negative visualization

This is similar to self-denial but is more drastic. The good news is that it only happens in your mind --- just in your imagination. So, how does this work? You will have to imagine losing all your loved ones. Yes, see them dying or already dead. Take note that this exercise can make you feel very sad. Some people who have tried it ended up in tears. The good news is that the bad things only happen in your imagination. The moment that you open your eyes, you will realize more the beauty of life and appreciate your loved ones more completely.

Tip:

Make the visualization as real as possible. Feel it. If you want to cry, then do not be shy to do so. The more that you internalize the visualization, the better it will be. Although Stoics discourage entertaining bad or negative thoughts, this exercise is one exception to that rule. Take note that this is just an exercise, and the aim of which is to make you a better person.

So, how can you benefit from this? If you do this exercise properly and seriously, then you will be more able to appreciate your loved ones. If you still feel sad even after the exercise, then do not be shy to go to your loved ones and embrace them.

This exercise is not limited to visualizing your loved ones. You can also apply it to your favorite material things. An important point of this exercise is to be able to appreciate something or someone more fully. Unfortunately, many people take things for granted, even their loved ones. With this exercise or meditation, you will be able to awaken your senses and realize what truly matters in your life.

Technic #4

A view from above

This is another common meditation in Stoicism based on the teaching of Marcus Aurelius: "You can rid yourself of many useless things among those that disturb you, for they lie entirely in your imagination; and you will then gain for yourself ample space by comprehending the whole universe in your mind, and by contemplating the eternity of time, and observing the rapid change of every part of everything, how short is the time from birth to dissolution, and the illimitable time before birth as well as the equally boundless time after dissolution."

So, how does it work? Well, you simply have to look at yourself from a third-party perspective by gradually zooming out your attention. You can start by looking at yourself right now and seeing your body just like any other body. Know that you are not the body. Next, zoom out a bit and focus on the room that you are in. Look around you. Now, zoom out again and imagine your whole house. Again, zoom out and imagine the whole city, and then your country, and then gradually zoom out up to the whole earth. This does not stop here. Realize that the earth is only a small part of the universe and that you compose an even smaller part of it. Again, zoom out and include the stars and other planets. Continue to zoom out until you get to imagine the entire universe. By doing this exercise, you will not only appreciate the beauty of the universe but also begin to see just how trivial your problems in life are. If someone insults you or hurts your feelings, try this exercise and you will realize that there is no good reason for you to be affected by the bad actions of the other person. Once you get this perspective, you will realize just how shallow are some of the emotions that you feel, and you will be more able to control them.

Technic #5

Voluntary discomfort

Epictetus taught that "Neither a bull nor a noble-spirited man comes to be what he is all at once; he must undertake hard winter training, and prepare himself, and not propel himself rashly into what is not appropriate to him."

So, for this exercise, you will intentionally put yourself through some uncomfortable situations. For example, sleeping on the floor, taking a cold shower, or skipping a meal. Many people are biased when it comes to receiving comfort but remain a stranger to discomfort when such should not be the case, as according to the Stoics. They believe that once you do not depend so much on comfort, life will be much easier for you. To do this, you need to have a relationship with comfort itself. To do this, you also need to get used to discomfort. Do not be afraid to get out of your comfort zone.

Reflect and apply

It is worth noting that these exercises are not something that you should do as a routine. To get the most out of these exercises and meditations, you need to reflect upon each and every of them and be sure to apply any new learning in your life precisely. Take note that true application denotes taking positive actions.

Also remember, that when you reflect, it is the time for you to be alone --- a time when you go into your inner sanctuary to ponder, and wonder. Now, some people think that to reflect, you need to get a break from your work schedule and go to a peaceful place, of course this may help, but it is not required. The best sanctuary can be found within yourself. You can go there every night as you are lying in bed or during your free time. Here is another teaching from Marcus Aurelius that can help enlighten you more on this matter: "People seek retreats for themselves in the countryside by the seashore, in the hills, and you too have made it your habit too long for that above all else. But this is altogether unphilosophical, when it is

171

possible for you to retreat into yourself whenever you please; for nowhere can one retreat into greater peace or freedom from care than within one's own soul, especially when a person has such things within him that he merely has to look at them to recover from that moment perfect ease of mind (and by ease of mind I mean nothing other than having one's mind in good order). So, constantly grant yourself this retreat and so, renew yourself; but keep within you concise and basic precepts that will be enough, at first encounter, to cleanse you from all distress and to send you back without discontent to the life to which you will return."

Another thing that you should do is to take note of interesting quotes from your favorite Stoics, and then spend some time to ponder about the teachings. Try to mix it with your meditations. For example, in Seneca's simple teaching that says, "If you would be loved, love." Reflect upon it and think of what you can do to be able to apply it in your life. In our given example, it says that you should love. Now, ask yourself, how can you love? How do you express it to someone? Also, come up with a plan composed of positive actions that you will take in order to convert the teachings into real actions. After all, the true meaning of Stoicism lies in actual application. The good news is that there are so many Stoic teachings that you can reflect upon. Do not hurry and take your time to really meditate upon the teachings.

It is also worth mentioning that Stoicism is not limited to the teachings of Aurelius, Epictetus, and Seneca. Even today, in the modern world, there are Stoics out there from whom you can also learn. In fact, you can even come up with your own Stoic teachings and practices. The important thing is not to let go of the fundamentals, such as living a virtuous life and not living in fear. Reflect in order to realize the true lesson behind the words, and apply in order to be a true Stoic and live a life that is full of peace and happiness. Study

Take it a step further and get hold of the writings of Seneca, Epictetus, and Marcus Aurelius. You can also get them for free online. They have many interesting teachings. Make sure to read the commentaries made by other writers and also come up with your own reflections and understanding. There are also many interesting websites and blogs on Stoicism that you can find online. You can also learn from them. Take note that the spirit of Stoicism continues to grow.

Live life to the fullest

Stoicism teaches that we should live life to the fullest without fear. No matter what your current situation in life is, then it is time for you to apply the Stoic teachings and face your life. Unfortunately, there are many people who hide or run away from their life. They cower away from living their dreams and continue to live the life that they do not want. It is time for you to break free from your shell and live fully. Be a Stoic and live without fear.

Lets Summarize the Chapter:

To the Stoics, peace does not depend on external things. Do not bother about what the outside world thinks or says about you. Remember, it is out of your control. If you allow other people to direct your path, then it would be impossible for you to find peace.

According to Epictetus, "Man is not worried by real problems so much as by his imagined anxieties about real problems." If you want to minimize stress and have a more peaceful mindset, then you should take control of your thoughts. Stop worrying too much. Take the effort to master your thoughts and think of more positive things.

You need to limit your exposure to stressful situations. A good way to do this is by giving just enough time to think about your problems. After which you should only entertain positive thoughts.

175

Another way to achieve peace of mind is by practicing meditation.

It is your perception of things that can make a big difference. Let go of anxiety and other negative thoughts and emotions.

Realize the truth that peace is within you. You only need to look within and recognize it. Control what you can and let go of those that are outside of your control.

Read and implement all the practical exercises and meditations. To get the most out of them, you need to reflect upon each and every of them and be sure to apply any new learning in your life precisely. Take note that true application denotes taking positive actions.

Remember, when you reflect, it is the time for you to be alone --- a time when you go into your inner sanctuary to ponder, and wonder. The best sanctuary can be found within yourself.

Take note of interesting quotes from your favorite Stoics, and then spend some time to ponder about the teachings. Try to mix it with your meditations. Come up with a plan composed of positive actions that you will take in order to convert the teachings into real actions

Do not hurry and take your time to really meditate upon the teachings.

Always remember that Stoicism is not limited to the teachings of Aurelius, Epictetus, and Seneca. Even today, in the modern world, there are Stoics out there from whom you can also learn.

Reflect in order to realize the true lesson behind the words, and apply in order to be a true Stoic and live a life that is full of peace and happiness.

Stoicism teaches that we should live life to the fullest without fear. It is time for you to break free from your shell and live fully. Be a Stoic and live without fear.

Let's take a close look at that sentence; we regret what we don't have. It doesn't seem entirely unusual at first, conjures up what seems a coherent and relatable idea at first glance. Or at least it conjures up a state of mind that we can relate to. I regret, for instance, that I didn't take more STEM classes when I was in college. Every new development in physics or cell biology baffles me a little. I don't have a strong background in the basics of those sciences to understand all the implications of the discovery. At what point does regret over a past failure transfer to the present? I regret that in my present moment I don't have a strong STEM background

I also regret, for that matter, that I don't have the money to buy a Tesla, that S model I hear is pretty amazing, goes zero to sixty in a few seconds, and you don't hear anything. I also regret that I didn't ask a certain person to marry me twenty years ago. Man, I feel like crap. I'm still driving a

Corolla, and my marriage was a disaster. If I get a Tesla—I could probably just barely make the payments, that is if I gave up food for two weeks every month, it's doable—maybe I'd look better to that intriguing new lady who just moved next door.

Yet regret also sneaks its way into the future. I regret that I won't ever have better STEM knowledge or that Tesla. We're getting into the crazy country here.

Regrets evidently come in a few different varieties. There's regret for actions omitted as well as actions taken. There's also, evidently, a more general regret that can include all those things I don't have that I would like to have. And that's where we can begin to see most clearly the absurd nature of regret in the first place. Don't think advertisers and marketers aren't deeply aware of this either. How many pitches are made that aim directly at this sense of general regret? A lot, if you look closely. You don't have a Tesla, do you? Well that's a problem, right? It's only the coolest car in the world. Do you know what it feels like to get to sixty miles per hour in three seconds? What's wrong with you?

What is regret anyway? Put simply it's lament or remorse over something that happened or didn't happen, in the past. That's bad enough, wasting time and energy ruminating over unchangeable past events. Yet somehow tricky little childish emotions, those fear-driven but intrepid toddlers of our triangle, just seem to take over and project themselves into our present moments of actual life. And boy they just make a big mess of things as toddlers do. They even, somehow, seem to be able to project themselves into the future. And that's really crazy. I so deeply regret that I will not own a Tesla in the future. It just breaks my heart. Yep, that's crazy.

Regret doesn't seem to be a very useful state of mind. Even when it's performing its prescribed dictionary function, lamenting something in the past, it just doesn't seem to get me anywhere I truly want to go. I really want to stay in the middle of my triangle. I've already determined that's it not only where I'm the most content, but it's also where I'm most useful to everyone around me. People like me most when I'm there. The center of the triangle is where life happens.

So how do we get rid of regret, and its playmates' lament and remorse? Well, we've just taken a gigantic step in doing so. We've identified it, unmasked them as the devilish little toddlers they are. Goodbye, regret, lament, and remorse. Have a nice nap.

Well, they'll be back, they'll pop up from their nap again. But after a while, they will learn to behave.

Wow. I think I just controlled something. I sent the fear-driven children away. I think I'm thinking a little more clearly now. What exactly did I do? Well first off I gave the noisy little toddlers of my fear-based emotions a name. I identified something and described it clearly. I saw how it was bothering me, not doing me any good, taking me away from the center of the triangle, which, by the way, I also thought my way into clearly articulating.

So what is within our power to control and what isn't?

When we form this question, we've landed right smack dab in the middle of Stoic philosophy, and we're putting it to work in or life. We're at the key entry point of our triangle, using our rational minds to observe not only the world around us but the world within us. It's within that world within us, of course, where we can exert significant measures of control. The world that exists apart from us may or may not conform to our wishes, mostly it won't happen in fact, but the world within us is where we truly live anyway. Remember the old adage—anytime I'm disturbed, the problem is within me.

And yet still the world around us runs wild, like a billion toddlers set loose to do exactly as they please it seems at times. Unfortunately, hardly any of them are my toddlers, who are happily napping right now. The analogy breaks down a little here. Lisa's boss, who didn't give her that promotion; Joseph's girlfriend who dumped him; Don's brother John, who may or may not see things as Don does, none of them are toddlers of course. Yet they all are forces that are out of the direct control of the people they're affecting, the unhappy protagonists of our three stories.

Yet they're all also people that must be reckoned with by our protagonists. Stoic principles, practiced daily, will help guide them in doing so. None any more so than, again, our favorite old adage, anytime something disturbs me, the problem is within me.

If we draw our boundaries carefully and clearly to just that point where we end, and the world begins, and strive to keep good order within our boundaries, our sense of well-being becomes not only untouchable; we begin to be able to experience love truly. We, at the very least, become most useful to those around us. Whether they see it or not, it is entirely beside the point. This isn't to say that we have the power to the right the world's wrongs. Let's be clear. We don't have that superpower. But we do contribute in positive and constructive ways that become a virtuous and self-reinforcing cycle both within us and in the world we live in. We strive to harmonize the two. Therein, say all the great sages, we begin to live.

Okay, so you're ready to sign up. That's great. First off, don't look for any thanks. So rather than that's great, let me rather say who cares as lesson number one. The world mostly doesn't care what your motivations are—why you've made a decision to practice Stoic principles in your daily life. Really, it just doesn't matter to anyone but you. Just like nobody's ill opinion of you should disturb you, neither should anyone's praise lift you up. Well, if you're married, there may be some minor, technical exceptions.

The point is if we're embarking on a program of self-mastery that results in a life of useful and harmonious well-being, and it's something you do because you want to because you've seen firsthand the futility of living a life based upon ego and self-centered motives. It just hasn't worked out. Time and time again, you've run up against some brick wall or another. Or when you've won life's lotteries, gotten that great thing you thought was the answer to all your problems, you found out it wasn't all that great, that it failed to fill some deeper spiritual need. The fact is, day to day, life just isn't that great. It's all just a humdrum routine of mindless consumption, and nobody does I want them to do, and then it's all over.

Okay, let's start. Let's break away from all that.

Let's get free.

CHAPTER 16: DEALING WITH NEGATIVE EMOTIONS

Stoics are capable of managing their emotions pretty well. Some individuals can attest that before they discovered and learn more about stoicism, they were plagued by particular teenage angst that most of the experience. Meditations by Marcus Aurelius also play a part in these experiences.

Though some individuals have not been cured of negative emotions and feelings and still experienced lows, stoicism has given them tools to deal with these.

Stoics are individuals who don't give a care to stupid things in the world that many individuals care about. Stoics have emotions but just fir things that do matter in this world. Stoics are one of the most real individuals alive.

Stoic Believes that Life Isn't Easy

When life becomes tough, stoics will not tell you to be happy and cheer up if you are feeling down. They won't tell you to be more positive either. The truth is, they will propagate the opposite. They also believe that you should try having hope for the future but eradicate this instead. For Stoics, hope is a heroine of emotions, and that higher one is lifted, the deeper he will fall.

Stoics would usually tell you something negative will happen, and that includes your partner leaving you, your car being hijacked, ending up in prison and many other bad things. But things will be okay. Stoics would tell you that life is full of misfortunes and you will get through it.

They also declare that negative feelings and emotions are the results of wrong judgments and that individuals expectations for realities weren't correct, and they should live in accordance with the truth or reality.

For the stoics, the good mental condition is identified by its virtue and capacity to reason out. There is this unanimous belief within the stoic community and that individuals should not be driven by emotions but by rationality instead. But this does not necessarily mean stamping out emotions altogether. This means getting rid of emotions out of the driver's seat and positioning them into the passengers' seat.

The belief of living in proper accordance with nature is probably controversial in the hedonistic modernity. This implies that foods are strictly for health and survival and sex, mainly for reproduction. They believed that having material goods will end up possessing them and that the more things you purchased, the higher the level of worrying about maintaining these things.

According to Marcus Aurelius, almost no material is needed for a happier life for one has fully understood existence. Believing in suicide is even more controversial. Stoics believed that a person must be allowed to take his own life.

When Seneca was asked to take his life by committing suicide, he did not even bat an eye. And while his children and wife hold firmly into him crying, he declared calmly that there is no need to cry over aspects of life for the entirety of life calls for these tears.

Seneca once said: "Can you no longer see a road to freedom? It's right in front of you. You need only turn over your wrists. "— Seneca

Now that you have learned more about stoics' belief, you might now be wondering how these can be applied in your life. The following information reveals some of the techniques used by stoics.

Stoics Equipment-The Tools in Living a Much Better Life

If you also wanted to live a much better life as you embrace stoicism, the following tools can help you accomplish this:

Negative Visualization

This pertains to the act of imagining the loss of what matters to you. It's often used by stoics to get rid of their fear for loss and to reduce the impacts when a loss happens. If you are that afraid and bothered about losing your spouse, imagine that he or she already left you. In any case, you are also afraid of losing your most valued car; imagine that you have just crashed your vehicle to the pole. If you are worried and afraid of losing money, then imagine living in the streets. And then ask yourself, is this the condition that you fear.

The premise of negative visualization imagines the loss of a lot of things, and when these occur, there will be less emotional impacts. You'll have expected it already for the reason that despite real efforts to avoid bad things, these happen. According to Seneca, misfortune weighs heavily on individuals who expect nothing but good fortunes.

Most individuals have lived in hedonic adaptations wherein they chase their desires only to realize that they have adapted to a new state and have more desires now. Negative visualization tends to reverse the process of hedonic adaptions. Rather than aiming for things that you do not have, negative visualization helps you desire the things that you already have. Visualizing loss of limb, loss of material goods or partner, a particular gratitude towards them.

Stoics asserted that during the time's, individuals are enjoying their loved ones. They need to periodically reflect on possibilities that existence of loved ones will disappear. Epictetus give them a piece of advice that whenever they kiss a child, keep in mind that this child was given to them for present and not inseparably or forever. Individuals should also reflect on possibilities that their fondness and enjoyment with the child are meant to end.

Worry Only on Things that You Can Control

Epictetus proclaimed that the most imperative choice in life is deciding whether to involve and concern yourself with internal and external. Most individuals choose external. They believe that their environment displays what's bad and what's good.

Stoics also believed that all harm and benefits come from within and that individuals should give up the rewards of the external world to achieve freedom, calmness and tranquility. Desire, by default, makes individuals unhappy for the reason that they wanted something that they do not have. The desire and happiness for what's present are impossible.

Techniques they've used in managing such unforgiving truth are changing their desires and not the world around them. In order to convince themselves out of the desires in their environments, stoics pronounced that their major desires must be able to prevent frustrations from developing desires that they cannot fulfill.

193

This idea was illustrated by Epictetus using a model named Dichotomy of Control. This is simple truth forgotten. Some things are really up to us, and certain things are not. Just focus on the things that you are in control.

Offer Yourself into Fate

Most individuals expect for things they want in this world. When these expectations do not come true, it might feel like the universe is not in favor. Stoics advised individuals to take fate or reality as they go along. Epictetus reminded individuals that they are actors in a play that is written by fate. People cannot choose the role they will play so instead of wanting things that did not happen, desire for the events to happen. According to Seneca, it's an excellent consolation that it's together with universe people have swept along.

Marcus Aurelius directed that something else would be defying nature. That individuals should love individuals that the destinies have bestowed upon them, welcome whatever obligations fall into them and acknowledge reality as they go. Remember, this is a similar man who invested most of his energy and effort for wars he needed to fight.

Reflection

Seneca states that individuals ought to intermittently consider the day by day events that have occurred and how they can improve (concurs intensely with the personal growth genre). He obtained this idea from Sextius, his teacher, who announced that he would cross-examine his mind with a similar inquiry:

"What illness of yours have you relieved or cured today? What failing have you stood up to? Where would you be able to demonstrate improvement?"

When he was excessively forceful in criticizing somebody, as opposed to proclaiming the individual for being powerless willed or weak-willed, he offered himself guidance. He decided that he somehow happened to give valuable analysis; he shouldn't just consider whether the analysis is substantial as well as think about whether the individual can stand being condemned or criticized.

It would be best to have some time doing some self-reflection taking, for instance, when writing into your diary. Ask yourself what you are grateful for today? How can you have improved today?

We have a long way to learn from stoics. A significant number of their strategies for carrying on with a solid passionate life can be connected every day. Their common sense and well-grounded frame of mind never stop to amaze people.

Emotion Control

People love power and feeling incredible and powerful. They respect stories of fortitude of individuals who face their adversaries and difficulties triumphantly as if they were Hercules. People might want to feel, in the event that they could, as the strong cliff which faces the ferocious seas and oceans without even moving and without giving in even a bit. It's possible. Individuals can encapsulate that control.

Individuals need to see, however, what that power is and how to utilize it. Stoicism is usually represented as a way of thinking or a philosophy with one major aim, and it is suppression or concealment of feeling, prominently accepted. It depicts stoics as a bit of iron or wood, fearless yet emotionless instead. This does not remain constant for Stoicism. Stoics are, toward the day's end, individuals charged with shyness, fear and love and humans to humans. The point of Stoicism isn't to suppress feeling; it is to live admirably well.

Emotion

An emotional condition of cognizance where delight, distress, dread, abhor, or the like, is experienced, as recognized from volitional and psychological conditions and states of consciousness.

There is no chance to get where individuals can't feel the emotion; feelings emerge. On the off chance that you happen to be in the subway amid the night and somebody hauls out a weapon, you will be apprehensive; you can't control not being afraid. Something very similar occurs with each circumstance throughout everyday life. When you have a crucial meeting, you will feel somewhat anxious, and if asking a lady out? Well, you might feel anxious and on edge also.

What Stoics contended with about feelings and emotions is that you don't need to stifle them, but instead, you should act in manners that give you the good ones and dodge the negative ones. You don't need to feel remorseful about feeling angry or afraid. The ascent of feeling is something that isn't under your immediate control. Thus this also turns out to be part of being indifferent.

Indifference means everything that isn't under individuals' immediate control. People must be cautiously mindful of what it is and what isn't that is under their immediate control. Feelings have a dubious impact, since they are the ones feeling it, and they also feel rulers of their emotions since they are feeling them literally. However, they cannot truly control the next emotion of thought that arises.

Practicing stoics, in any case, has the limit of applied reasons. Volition is the ability to exert will. It is in the ability to apply own will where one can end up like the unmoving rock amidst the waves. The feeling may rise, yet it is exposed to our reason and cardinal ethics: the knowledge, justice, courage and temperance.

Stoically, individuals can ignore interests as indifferent, yet at the same time, feel the entire circle of feelings and emotions without limitations; it is in this power, where individuals have emotion control.

Ensure that rulings and sovereign piece of your spirit and soul stay unaffected by each movement, violent or smooth, in your flesh and that it doesn't consolidate with them, yet encircles itself, and limits these encounters to bodily parts. At whatever point they communicate themselves into the mind utilizing virtue of the other sympathy, as will undoubtedly happen unified organisms, you shouldn't try resisting the temptations which are considered natural ones. However, you should not allow the ruling center of adding its own and further judgments that experiences are bad or good.

You can feel dread, yet act with mental fortitude at any rate.

You can feel disgrace and shame, yet stand gladly anyway.

You can feel outraged or anger, yet always act with justice.

Action and stoicism go hand in hand. Stoics don't wait, and he acts no matter what. The more the difficulties, the more noteworthy for the Stoic personality and mind because for this can practice its power of overcoming it.

Epictetus also said:

"The greater the difficulty, the more glory in surmounting it. Skillful pilots gain their reputation from storms and tempests. "

Also, the notable difference between a wise man and fool man depends on the power of putting everything that he experiences into a test for his reasons and then act accordingly.

CONCLUSION

I am so happy that you chose this book as your guide on your way to becoming a stoic. This book covered the practical aspects of the topic. The exercises can be a serious step towards your goal. This philosophy makes you a better human being. You learn how to deal with various situations. In turn, your life gets better with stoicism. Stoicism helps you to be able to carry yourself in a better way, whether it is emotionally or mentally. The more real you become by adapting stoicism, the easier it becomes for you to create a life that others dream about.

Don't forget to continue your stoic education beyond this book. Read the works of the great philosophers, discover their wisdom for yourself, and immerse your mind in the virtues and teachings of brilliant minds who came before. Many others have been on this journey before you. It would be wise to take a page from their book (perhaps literally) and see how you can apply stoicism in your everyday life. It is only with constant practice that we get better at anything, including philosophy.

CPSIA information can be obtained
at www.ICGtesting.com
Printed in the USA
BVHW041347280121
598991BV00010B/548

9 781989 744772